IN SEARCH OF
JAPAN'S HIDDEN
CHRISTIANS

Also by John Dougill:

Gentlemen and Hooligans: The British in Film, 1921–1971
Kyoto: A Cultural History
Oxford in English Literature

IN SEARCH OF JAPAN'S HIDDEN CHRISTIANS

A STORY OF SUPPRESSION, SECRECY AND SURVIVAL

JOHN DOUGILL

TUTTLE Publishing

Tokyo | Rutland, Vermont | Singapore

The Tuttle Story: "Books to Span the East and West"

Most people are very surprised to learn that the world's largest publisher of books on Asia had its beginnings in the tiny American state of Vermont. The company's founder, Charles E. Tuttle, belonged to a New England family steeped in publishing. And his first love was naturally books—especially old and rare editions.

Immediately after WW II, serving in Tokyo under General Douglas MacArthur, Tuttle was tasked with reviving the Japanese publishing industry, and founded the Charles E. Tuttle Publishing Company, which still thrives today as one of the world's leading independent publishers.

Though a westerner, Charles was hugely instrumental in bringing a knowledge of Japan and Asia to a world hungry for information about the East. By the time of his death in 1993, Tuttle had published over 6,000 titles on Asian culture, history and art—a legacy honored by the Japanese emperor with the "Order of the Sacred Treasure," the highest tribute Japan can bestow upon a non-Japanese.

With a backlist of 1,500 books, Tuttle Publishing is as active today as at any time in its past—inspired by Charles' core mission to publish fine books to span the East and West and provide a greater understanding of each.

Published by Tuttle Publishing, an imprint of Periplus Editions (HK) Ltd.

www.tuttlepublishing.com

Copyright © 2012 by John Dougill

Library of Congress Cataloging-in-Publication Data

Dougill, John.
 In search of Japan's hidden Christians : a story of suppression,
secrecy, and survival / John Dougill. —1st ed.
   p. cm.
 Includes bibliographical references.
 ISBN 978-4-8053-1147-9 (hardcover)
 1. Crypto-Christians—Japan. 2. Japan—Church history. 3.
Christianity—Japan. 4. Catholic Church—Japan—History. I. Title.
 BX1668.D68 2012
 282'.5209—dc23
           2011027419

ISBN 978-4-8053-1147-9

Distributed by

North America, Latin America & Europe
Tuttle Publishing
364 Innovation Drive
North Clarendon, VT 05759-9436 U.S.A.
Tel: 1 (802) 773-8930; Fax: 1 (802) 773-6993
info@tuttlepublishing.com
www.tuttlepublishing.com

Japan
Tuttle Publishing
Yaekari Building, 3rd Floor, 5-4-12 Osaki
Shinagawa-ku, Tokyo 141 0032
Tel: (81) 3 5437-0171; Fax: (81) 3 5437-0755
sales@tuttle.co.jp
www.tuttle.co.jp

Asia Pacific
Berkeley Books Pte. Ltd.
61 Tai Seng Avenue #02-12
Singapore 534167
Tel: (65) 6280-1330; Fax: (65) 6280-6290
inquiries@periplus.com.sg
www.periplus.com

First edition
16 15 14 13 12
10 9 8 7 6 5 4 3 2 1   1110RP

Printed in China

For the late Hal Gold, who first gave me the idea

"In Japanese history there is no more attractive or interesting period than that of the Kirishitan, especially as it makes us think about what it is to be a human being."

— Endo Shusaku (translated by Peter Milward)

Contents

A map showing the sites of these events can be found on page 2.

Preface

In 1549 the first Christian missionaries arrived in Japan. Over the next sixty years the mission managed to convert more than 300,000 Japanese to their belief, including some of the most powerful people in the country. But in the process they made enemies too, and in 1614 a nationwide ban was issued, followed by a vicious campaign of persecution. A religion that preached against the workings of evil was itself denounced as evil. Because it threatened the power of the shogun, torture and executions were used against believers as the authorities grew increasingly determined to make them recant. Over 4,000 people are known to have died for their faith, and thousands of others suffered misery and ruination. In 1639 the country was sealed to prevent "contagion" from the outside, and by the end of the next decade it seemed the religion had been eradicated from the country.

For over two hundred years Japan remained a closed society, except for Chinese traders and a handful of Dutch at Nagasaki. Only in 1854 was it prised open again. Eleven years later came an astonishing revelation: groups of villagers, mostly illiterate, had continued to practice Christianity in secret despite all the preventative measures put in place. For seven generations they had passed the religion down to their children despite having no Bible, no priests, and no sacraments except for baptism. Isolated and imperiled, they clung to their faith, and the result was often unorthodox. Remarkably, even after the toleration of Christianity, about half refused to rejoin the Catholic Church and carried on with the rituals and prayers taught to them as children. Some of their descendants still do.

On the other side of the world, a curious parallel to the Hidden Christians could be found in the secret Jews of the Iberian Peninsula. Ironically, Christians were doing the persecuting rather than being persecuted, and it was happening in the very countries from which the missionaries had left for Japan. When the Jews were ordered to convert to Catholicism or be expelled in 1492, it's thought that up to 200,000 subsequently became Marranos—Christian converts who were secret practitioners of Judaism. Some of the families continued the practice into modern times, and a documentary entitled *The Last Marranos* was made as late as 1997.

Like the Marranos, the Hidden Christians are bound up with issues that extend beyond religion to race and identity. In Japan's case, it had much to do with the clash of East and West, for the Confucian and Socratic traditions had produced different ways of thinking that were compounded by the contrast between East Asian polytheism and Christian monotheism. What happened when representatives of the two cultures first met? Having spent the greater part of my adult life in Japan, I was naturally intrigued by the question, and my interest was fueled by reading Endo Shusaku's compelling novel, *Silence* (1966). When I learned of the tenacity with which Japanese peasants had clung to the European faith, I couldn't help wondering what had motivated them to risk death and the ruination of their loved ones. In unpacking the answer to that question, I had the feeling that I would be picking at the very essence of the culture.

The coming of the missionaries to Japan has much in common with the spread of early Christianity. When Paul arrived in Corinth, there were well-established pagan deities and a huge temple to Apollo, the Sun God. When Francis Xavier arrived in Japan, there was not only a well-established religion in Buddhism but an array of native deities headed by Amaterasu, the Sun Goddess. Paul traveled around the Aegean, setting up groups that met in private houses and to whom he addressed long letters. Xavier and his fellow missionaries did much the same thing, writing long reports on their activities back to Rome. In both cases the religion won a following by offering dignity to the dispossessed and salvation in a world to come. For societies in which most of the population was downtrodden and desperate, the message of spiritual equality proved liberating.

For those in power, the message was anything but liberating: it was threatening. In Rome believers refused to participate in pagan festivities or public sacrifices to the emperor. In Japan allegiance to the Church clashed with allegiance to the shogun. In both cases the religion came to be seen as subversive, resulting in persecution and crucifixion. One vital difference was the conversion of Constantine in the early fourth century, following which Christianity was able to flourish. Japan too almost had its Constantine moment, but when it failed to materialize, things developed in a very different direction and Hidden Christians became the faith's last refuge.

In mulling over why they had risked so much for an imported faith, I came to see the Hidden Christians in terms of a mirror image. Here was I, a European interested in Japanese spirituality: they on the other hand were Japanese attracted to a European religion. As I came to "reflect" on the nature of the mirror, I felt a compulsion to see for myself the cutting edge of the culture clash that had taken place. In this way I would surely come to understand more fully the country in which I had chosen to make my home. In short, I was hoping to do more than uncover Hidden Christians: I was hoping to journey deeper into Japan, past and present.

But if I was to go in search of Hidden Christians, it had to be done soon, for surviving practitioners were few in number. Writing in 2003, Miyazaki Kentaro estimated that there were only 1,000 to 1,500 practitioners left, most of whom were elderly. Because of a lack of interest by the younger generation, there was no fresh blood and baptisms had all but stopped. Clearly, there was little time to waste, but where was I to start? The obvious answer was at the very beginning, and so one fine day in 2010 I set out from my home in Kyoto for a faraway island of which I knew nothing. Like all good stories, the encounter of East and West had started with a chance happening.

Acknowledgments

Among the many people who rendered assistance, I'd like to express my gratitude to the people below for their help with feedback and input. My thanks to all of them. In addition, I would like to express appreciation for the unsung curators and academic advisors at the various collections that I visited in Kyushu and Azuchi, as well as the local guides. They were unfailingly kind and helpful, making the whole venture a pleasure from beginning to end.

Martin Repp, my former colleague at Ryukoku University, for casting an expert eye on the manuscript

Paul Carty and Julie Highmore for taking the time to read through chapters and offer advice

Roger Vanzila Munsi in the Faculty of Foreign Studies, Nanzan University, who helped with the Sotome chapter

Christal Whelan, who read through the Goto chapter

Kirk Sandvig, who gave feedback on the Goto and Sotome sections

Yuriko Suzuki, who acted as research assistant and chauffeur, as well as providing backup

Professor Higashibaba of Tenri University, who allowed me to attend his class and took the trouble to answer my questions

Miyazaki Kentaro, who spared time for me at his office in Nagasaki Junshin Catholic University

William Johnston, the translator of *Silence*, who answered questions following a talk he gave in Kyoto

Nakazono Shigeo of the the Ikitsuki Museum, who generously made time to guide me around the exhibition

Urabe Tomoyuki of the Hirado Museum, who was kind enough to answer questions and provide valuable contacts

Kawakami Shigetsugu, who devoted an afternoon to showing me around Neshiko and the Hirado Christian Museum

Timeline

Note: *Kirishitan* is a term used to refer to Catholics in Japan in the sixteenth and seventeenth centuries. Following the time of persecution, it was used in the expression *Kakure Kirishitan* (Hidden Christians).

1543	Portuguese arrive in Tanegashima
1547	Meeting of Anjiro and Francis Xavier in Malacca
1549	Francis Xavier arrives in Kagoshima with the first Japan mission
1559	Gaspar Vilela begins the Miyako mission (Kyoto)
1563	The first "Kirishitan daimyo" is baptised (Omura Sumitada)
1579	Arrival of Alessandro Valignano on his first visit
1580	Nagasaki ceded to the Jesuits by Omura Sumitada
1582	Departure of the Four Envoys for Rome
1587	Hideyoshi orders the expulsion of missionaries
1588	Nagasaki and Urakami placed under Hideyoshi's direct control
1590	Valignano arrives with the Four Envoys and a printing press
1593	Arrival of the Spanish Franciscans
1596	Shipwreck of the *San Felipe* off Shikoku
1597	26 Martyrs crucified at Nagasaki

1600	Arrival of William Adams on a Dutch ship (*Liefde*); Battle of Sekigahara
1601	The first Japanese are ordained to the priesthood
1602	Arrival of the Augustinians and Dominicans
1609	The Dutch factory (trading station) set up at Hirado
1612	The shogunate bans Christianity in its domains
1613	Establishment of the English factory at Hirado
1614	Statement expelling missionaries and nationwide ban on Christianity
1615	Defeat of Toyotomi rebels at Osaka Castle, including many Christians
1619	Great Kyoto Martyrdom (52 burned at the stake)
1623	Great Edo Martyrdom (50 burned at the stake); English factory at Hirado closes
1632	Great Genna Martyrdom in Nagasaki (55 martyred)
1634	Travel overseas banned for Japanese
1637–38	Shimabara Uprising in which 37,000 are massacred
1639	Final "closed country" edict. All Europeans expelled except for the Dutch
1641	Dutch moved to Dejima
1657	Kohri *kuzure* (persecution)
1790–95	First Urakami *kuzure*
1805	Amakusa *kuzure*
1842	Second Urakami *kuzure*
1853	Arrival of Commodore Perry's Black Ships
1854	Treaty with the United States and ending of isolationism
1856	Third Urakami *kuzure*
1859	Return of first Catholic missionaries (Paris Foreign Mission Society)
1865	Petitjean's meeting with Urakami Hidden Christians
1867–73	Fourth Urakami *kuzure*

1873	Signboards banning Christianity taken down; unofficial toleration
1880s	Differences arise between Catholics and "Separated Christians"
1895	Construction of Urakami Cathedral begins
1914	Urakami Cathedral commemorated
1945	Destruction of Urakami Cathedral by atomic bomb
1966	Endo Shusaku's *Silence*
1992	Disbanding of Neshiko Hidden Christian organization
1999	Establishment of Karematsu Jinja interfaith festival
2013	Proposed application for UNESCO World Heritage Site by Churches and Christian Sites in Nagasaki

Japanese Eras

Jomon (13,000 to c.300 BC) Hunter-gatherers, fishing and pottery

Yayoi (c.300 BC–c.300 AD) Rice culture, iron, independent "countries," and Himiko (shaman queen)

Kofun (c.300–538) Burial mounds; emergence of Yamato hegemony and emperor system

Asuka (538–710) Buddhism and Chinese influences; first constitution under Prince Shotoku

Nara (710–794) First "permanent capital." Building of Todaiji.

Heian (794–1186) An aristocratic age with rule by the emperor from Heian-kyo (Kyoto)

Kamakura (1186–1333) Beginning of samurai rule, with a military leader (shogun) in Kamakura

Muromachi (1333–1573) Ashikaga dynasty rules from Kyoto; central power collapses in Period of Warring States (Sengoku Period)

Azuchi-Momoyama (1573–1600) Unification under Nobunaga Oda and Hideyoshi Toyotomi

Edo (1600–1867) Tokugawa rule and an age of isolationism

Meiji (1868–1912) Restoration of the emperor in the newly named Tokyo. Westernization and modernization

Taisho (1912–26) Industrial growth and imperialism

Showa (1926–89) Militarism, World War Two, and the postwar economic miracle

Heisei (1989–present) Economic bubble; aging society and rural depopulation

Japanese Eras

In Search of
Japan's Hidden
Christians

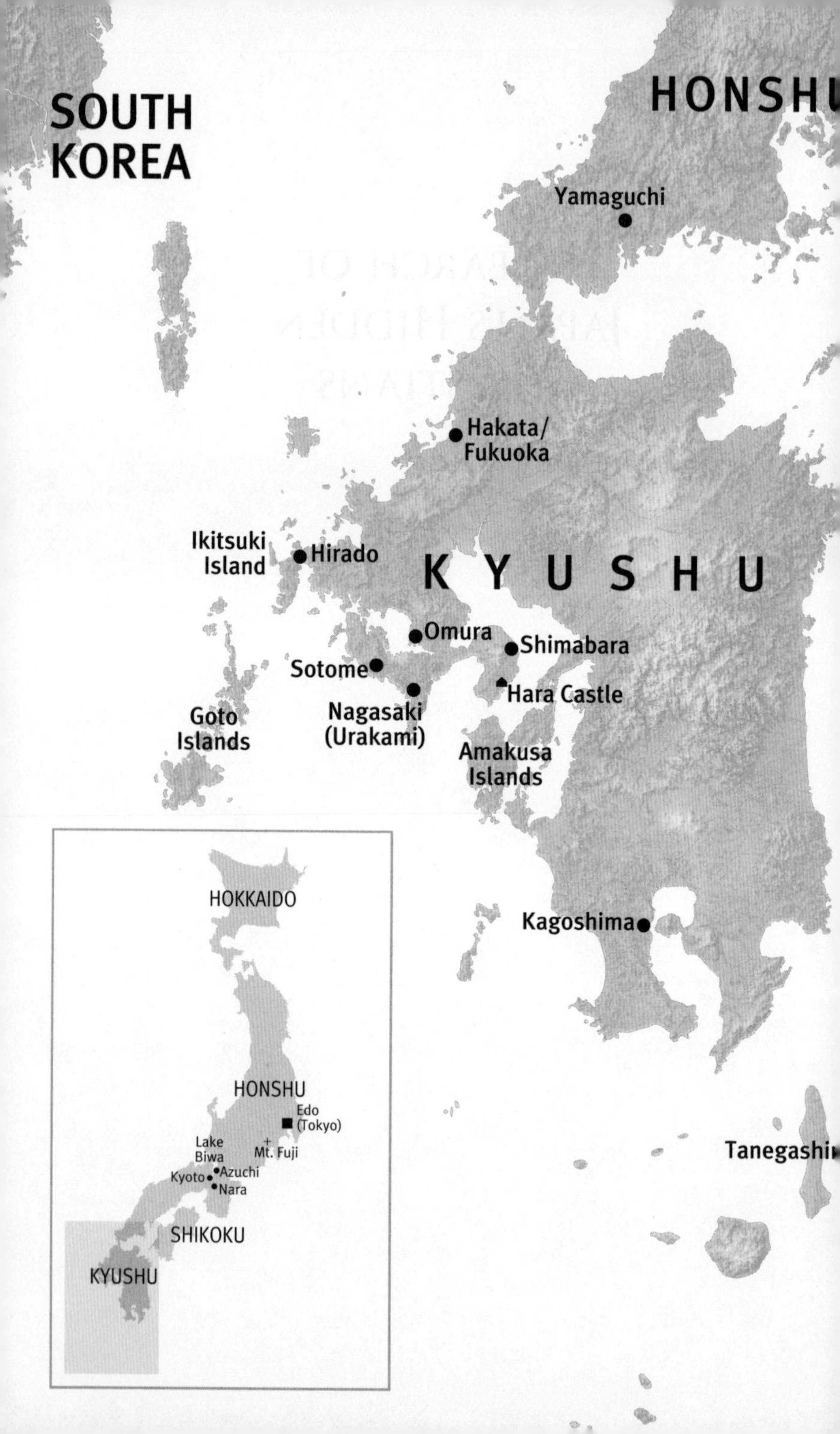

SOUTH KOREA

HONSHU

Yamaguchi

Hakata/
Fukuoka

Ikitsuki
Island

Hirado

K Y U S H U

Omura

Shimabara

Sotome

Hara Castle

Nagasaki
(Urakami)

Goto
Islands

Amakusa
Islands

Kagoshima

Tanegashi

HOKKAIDO

HONSHU

Edo
(Tokyo)

Lake
Biwa

Mt. Fuji

Kyoto

Azuchi

Nara

SHIKOKU

KYUSHU

Prelude
(Tanegashima)

Southern Barbarians

"You see where the beach ends?"

"Yes."

"And you see the stretch of rocks."

"Yes."

"That's where it happened. That's where the ship landed. Right there, according to island folklore."

We're standing on the southernmost tip of Tanegashima, Japan's sixth biggest island. It lies to the south of Kyushu, in the direction of Okinawa. In front of us a pleasant bay stretches away into the distance, the blue of the sea offset by golden sand and a green-tinged shoreline. This is where the South China Sea meets the Pacific. Westward lies the island of Yakushima and beyond it China; to the east, far, far away, America. There's no one else around on this sunny autumn morning, and a flock of *mejiro* are chirping noisily among the nearby trees. Surprisingly, my guide and I have this scenic site all to ourselves.

The ship we're talking about is the one that brought the first Europeans to Japan. They arrived in 1543 in the form of two (possibly three) Portuguese merchants aboard a Chinese junk.

The ship was making its way along the coast of China for trading purposes when it was blown off course by a vicious storm, during which it was badly damaged and no longer able to steer a course. Left to drift with the prevailing current, it was deposited in this welcoming bay at Cape Kadokura. In this way, through the whims of the weather, history was made.

A scaled-down replica of the junk stands on the headland, and you can see why it would have wanted to hug the coastline, for the curious box-like shape must have stood high in the water and was clearly unsuited to ocean-going. The original, some two hundred to three hundred tons in size, had approximately one hundred men on board, no doubt squeezed into cramped conditions. When it was seen by the locals, there was great excitement and the village head was summoned to talk to the captain. Though they had no common language, they were able to communicate by drawing Chinese characters in the sand. The odd clothing, large eyes and "high noses" of the exotic Europeans soon aroused interest, for the Japanese had seen nothing like them. They not only looked different but behaved differently, and in response to questions the villagers were told that the men were "Southern Barbarians." The name derived from the Chinese custom of calling all foreigners barbarians, distinguished only by the direction from which they came. (The Portuguese had arrived from Malacca in western Malaya.)

At the time, Japan lay on the outermost edge of European consciousness. Ever since Marco Polo wrote of the great gold rumored to be in Zipangu, it had held a fascination for explorers, and though Christopher Columbus made it one of his objectives, his voyages had taken him to other shores. Not long afterwards, Spain and Portugal divided up the world under the Treaty of Tordesillas (1494). A line down the Atlantic separated the colonial powers: Spain took everything to the west, Portugal to the east. South America (apart from Brazil) fell into the Spanish sphere, and Asia belonged to the Portuguese. Accordingly, as Spanish conquistadors battled Aztecs and Incas, the Portuguese made their way around the coasts of Africa and across the Indian Ocean. In 1498 Vasco de Gama reached India for the first time, and in 1510 his compatriots seized Goa. The following year they captured Malacca. By 1513 they had arrived in China, and by 1521 the Philippines. It seemed just a matter of time before they reached Japan. The surprise is that it took so long.

When the arrival of the Chinese junk was reported to the fifteen-year-old lord of Tanegashima, he ordered the villagers to tow the ship to the main port in the north of the island. The crew was put up in a temple while an assessment of the ship was made. Attention was soon aroused by the peculiar long firearms the Portuguese had, and a demonstration was arranged at which the target was hit from a distance of some hundred yards. To borrow a phrase, it was a shot that was heard around Japan. Western technology had arrived with a bang.

The colorful adventurer Mendes Pinto (c.1509–83) wrote a self-aggrandizing memoir for his children in which he described being "thirteen times made captive and seventeen times sold" in exploits that ranged from Ethiopia to the Far East. Among his claims was that of being on the Tanegashima junk, and in his account he wrote that the local lord had been presented with a musket in return for his hospitality after being impressed by the Portuguese shooting ducks. However, the memoirs are known to be unreliable, and it is almost certain that Pinto went to Japan on a later ship and wanted to write himself into the discovery of the country. The similarity of Mendes with *mendacious* has not gone unnoticed.

Realizing the power of the new weapon, the Tanegashima lord immediately ordered the making of a copy. He was able to do this because there was already a concentration of smiths on the island, thanks to the "black sand" on the beaches, which was rich in iron particles. The smiths had a reputation for high-quality swords and knives; even today Tanebasami is a brand name for handmade scissors, and Kyoto chefs still use Tanegashima knives for their exquisite *kaiseki* dishes. How long it took to complete the musket is uncertain, but after four months the young lord felt bold enough to seize control of the neighboring island. It's tempting to presume this was the first instance of gun law in Japan, but in his book *Tanegashima: The Arrival of Europe in Japan*, Olof Lidin supposes the musket was only perfected at a later date because of technical difficulties concerning the fitting of a screw. Thereby hangs an island tale, which my guide was eager to tell me.

"This is Wakasa," he said, pointing at a statue near the island's port. It showed a young woman in kimono with a musket nestled in her arms. "There are two versions of her story. One says that the smith making the musket could not manage to complete the job, so to get the information he needed about the screw he sold his daughter to a Portuguese man who came on a later ship. And then he could complete the musket. You know, he had responsibility to make a copy of the musket, so if he could not do that he must commit seppuku.

"But I prefer the romantic version," he went on with a laugh. "The romantic version is that a Portuguese man came and fell in love with her, and in gratitude for winning permission to take her away he gave the smith the information he needed. So we can say Wakasa had the first 'international marriage' with a Westerner."

There are many tales in Japan's past of poverty-stricken families committing infanticide or selling off their daughters, and it occurred to me poor Wakasa might well have had no choice in the matter. A later account written by an islander claims she was taken to Ningpo, a Portuguese enclave on the Chinese coast, but felt homesick and persuaded her husband to take her back with him on the next trip. Once rejoined with her family, she feigned death and arranged for a funeral in the hope that he would presume she had passed away. If the romance led to marriage, then marriage had killed the romance.

Whether the story is true or not, it's striking how the coupling of Western male and oriental female, the Madame Butterfly syndrome, seems to have kicked in from the very beginning. Western culture with its phallic muskets and technological orientation has often been characterized as masculine in its aggressive, outward-going nature. Eastern culture with its sensitivity, receptivity and inner cultivation has been characterized as feminine. The fascination of opposites was furthered by the physical differences, for the tall Europeans embodied the ideal of a well-built man, while the oriental female typified that of the petite woman. From the first encounter, the magnetic attraction between them found outlet in coupled union.

A key factor in the making of the Tanegashima musket had been the quality of the island's smiths, and I was introduced to one of the descendants still working in the trade. A genial soul of sixty-eight, he took me into his simple hut of a forge to demonstrate how to bash out a scissor-blade. It seemed simplicity itself, but as with all master craftsmen the ease belied the long years of training. When he told me he was the thirty-seventh generation of his family to do the work, I did a quick calculation and realized with a shock his family must have been smiths for about a thousand years. "More," he answered. "From the time of Emperor Kammu [737–806]."

Tragically, the smith was set to be the end of a long line, for neither of his two daughters nor their husbands were interested in taking over a hot, dirty and insolvent business. "You just get burned," he said with a laugh, showing me his blackened hands. The making of swords and guns had been forbidden in Meiji times, and after World War Two the import of cheap scissors dealt a death blow to what remained of the business. I felt upset for the stoical smith, but there were similar stories throughout the country as traditional practices came to the end of a line. The Hidden Christians too were said to be a dying breed. Beginnings and ends: Tanegashima had already provided both. Was that what this journey was about?

In the island museum are exhibits of one of the first Portuguese muskets together with a Japanese version. I noticed that the English explanation mistakenly reversed the identification, so that the original was described as a copy and vice versa, as if to imply the replica was so good that even museum staff couldn't tell them apart. As it happened, the Japanese did more than just copy the arquebus, for they later improved it with increased caliber, adjustable trigger pull, and waterproof cases for matchlocks and gunpowder. It was symptomatic of the ability to adopt and adapt that has served the country so well over the millennia.

Copies of the musket soon spread around Japan, and manufacture was started in other regions. Meanwhile, Portuguese ships continued to bring in fresh supplies, and gunfire came to play a part in samurai fighting. In 1575 at the Battle of Nagashino, the musket played a decisive part in open warfare for the first time, when the warlord Nobunaga used rotating volleys of fire to defeat his enemy. By the end of the century, it's said that Japan not only had the best guns in the world but the highest rate of ownership per capita. Even in the sixteenth century, the culture was quick to respond to technological innovation! Though personally I'd have reservations about celebrating such a dubious import, Tanegashima has proudly adopted the musket as its motif, and models are everywhere—in the lobby of the hotel where I stayed, in the restaurant I ate at, and even at the base of a torii (Shinto gateway) at Cape Kadokura.

The island has another claim to fame, for it also hosts Japan's foremost rocket site: NEAREST ISLAND TO THE MOON, say the tourist posters. Oddly enough, the space center is sited next to the bay where the Portuguese first landed, so that the first and latest examples of Western technology stand side by side, as it were. It seemed an extraordinary coincidence. "Maybe it's not coincidence," my guide responded . . .

"Maybe it happened because of the geography. You see, for the satellite launch it's preferable to have a southern island near the equator. It needs to be near the sea so as not to disturb people. And you need a friendly people. We get many visitors here from NASA, you see. People are very welcoming. Just as they welcomed the Portuguese. And they don't cause trouble. We didn't object to the space shuttle being sited here, though others might have objected. We're not like the farmers who fought against Narita airport," he added with a smile.

"And does the space center cause much disturbance?" I asked.

"Just twice a year when there's a rocket launch. Then the whole island knows about it. There's a great flash. And after comes a roaring noise and windows start rattling. Even the windows of the car vibrate. It's like an earthquake."

The next day as I left Tanegashima, I couldn't help but feel a tinge of regret, brief though my stay had been. It's not as popular as its mountainous neighbor Yakushima, whose ancient cedars and unique ecosystem make it a World Heritage Site. Tanegashima by contrast is relatively flat, drawing surfers to the breaking waves along its pleasant coastline. A peaceful place of 36,000 people, it produces sweet potato and sugarcane and enjoys a rich marine life thanks to the convergence of currents, which have long brought people from distant parts. Here on the island was found the oldest known rice in Japan, called *akamai* (red rice), which is probably Polynesian in origin and dates from Jomon times. Here too was found the oldest *kanji* (Chinese character), dating from the Yayoi period.

One imagines the Portuguese merchants were not unhappy in Tanegashima. It took two months to repair their junk, after which they sailed back to China, and when they reported on the attractions of the newly discovered country their compatriots hastily prepared an expedition. Six months later a Portuguese ship arrived in Kyushu to do trade, and thereafter "the China ship" from Macao was to make regular trips. The "great ship," as it came to be known, played a key role in the Catholic mission to Japan, and it was on one such ship that the man who became Japan's first Christian stowed away following a killing in which he was involved. His was a remarkable story, and it centered on his hometown of Kagoshima on the southern coast of Kyushu, to which I was now headed.

Chapter One

Genesis
(Kagoshima)

The Japanese and the Jesuit

Six years after the Tanegashima musket came the Bible. It was brought by Francisco Xavier (1506–52), "Apostle of the East" as he has been dubbed. Born into the Navarre aristocracy (the country was annexed by Spain while he was still a child), he was raised in a splendid castle that is now a tourist sight and destination for an annual pilgrimage. As a youth he went to study in Paris, where he proved himself a gifted scholar ahead of whom lay a promising career, but a chance meeting with Ignatius Loyola changed the course of his life. Under the Spaniard's direction, Xavier took to a disciplined regime of fasting and meditation. In 1540 he became one of the seven founding members of the Society of Jesus, more commonly known as the Jesuits.

Since the Christian mission to Japan was essentially a Jesuit affair (for over forty years they had a monopoly), it's worth considering the opening words of the organization's charter. It reflects the military background of Ignatius Loyola, who saw the group as a religious crack force at the service of the pope.

Whoever desires to serve as a soldier of God beneath
the banner of the cross in our Society, which we desire

to be designated by the name of Jesus, and to serve
the Lord alone and the Church, his spouse, under the
Roman pontiff, the vicar of Christ on earth, should,
after a solemn vow of perpetual chastity, poverty and
obedience, keep what follows in mind. He is a member of a Society founded chiefly for this purpose: to
strive especially for the defense and propagation of
the faith and for the progress of souls in Christian life
and doctrine.

The order was founded at a time when Catholicism was strug-
gling to come to terms with the Protestant Reformation (Martin
Luther had nailed his protest to the door of the Wittenberg
church in 1517). In the drive to reinvent itself, the Church found
a new sense of purpose and righteousness. Such were Loyola's
convictions that he famously said: "We should always be prepared
so as never to err to believe that which appears white is really
black, if the hierarchy of the Church so decides." It's an extraordinary remark, and one that sheds light on later developments.

The Jesuits were the first order to be organized specifically
for missionary work, and when the king of Portugal asked the
pope for a priest to accompany his ships to Goa, the task fell to
Xavier. He set sail on his thirty-fifth birthday. The voyage was a
perilous undertaking, for the large double-masted ships were
unstable and navigation was an inexact science. It was not unusual for up to half of the crew to die en route, so the boats were
deliberately overmanned, with six hundred to eight hundred
men. As well as sickness and storms, losses could be expected to
hostile encounters, onboard riots or simply the lure of foreign
parts. In Xavier's case the ship was delayed in Mozambique by
unfavorable winds, and the journey took some eighteen months.

During the voyage Xavier ministered to the crew despite frequent sea-sickness, and though he was invited to have a servant

and dine at the captain's table, he chose to share the conditions of the ordinary sailor. It was typical of the one-time aristocrat, who throughout his career lived as the poorest of men, eating little and sleeping on bare boards or the ground. He insisted too on walking everywhere, even when offered rides on horseback. There seems to have been a curious masochistic element to his zeal, for as well as scourging himself he wrote of pain as participation in the "sweetness" of the cross and he idealized crucifixion as a measure of God's love. The devotion is impressive, though the psychology puzzling.

Goa at this time was the Catholic base for the whole of Asia, with fourteen churches and 20,000 converts. As head of the mission, Xavier proved an indefatigable worker, preaching to the poor and caring for outcasts. He was concerned too about deviations from orthodoxy and wrote to the pope to urge an inquisition. He tried to spread God's word as widely as he could, traveling back and forth over the equator in his efforts. From Indonesian cannibals to Philippine poisoners, he showed a willingness to brave every type of danger if he thought there was a chance of spreading the word. One of the places his travels took him was the Portuguese enclave of Malacca, and it is at this point that a Japanese fugitive named Yajiro (also known as Angero) enters the story.

Whether Yajiro was a samurai or a merchant is uncertain, but involvement in a killing forced him to escape from Kagoshima on a Portuguese ship, along with two companions (one of whom may have been his younger brother). The ship delivered them to Macao, where in less than a year Yajiro was able to make himself understood in Portuguese. He developed an interest in the religion of the Europeans, and though his motives are unclear, it's an intriguing thought that he may have been driven by a guilty conscience and a wish for absolution. To deepen his understanding he was advised by a Portuguese captain to consult the well-informed priest at Malacca, and after traveling there by ship he managed to track Xavier down to a church where he was conducting a wedding. In their discussion he asked some probing questions and took notes, which impressed the missionary. "If all the Japanese are as eager to know as is Yajiro," he wrote in a report, "it seems to me that this race is the most curious of all the peoples that have been discovered."

Xavier encouraged Yajiro and his companions to go to Goa for further study, where they became the first ever Japanese Christians by being baptised in the cathedral. Yajiro, thirty-six by this time, took the name of Paolo; his companions became Antonio and Joane. With their Christian names, they became Westernized figures who stood halfway between the extreme west of Europe and the extreme east of Asia. How appropriate then that the ceremony should have taken place in India.

Meanwhile, Xavier had commissioned a report on Japan from a Portuguese captain, which confirmed that the people were educated, diligent and interested in new ideas. It seemed the country was ripe for missionary work. "I have with much interior satisfaction decided to go to this land," he wrote in a letter, "for it seems to me that a people of this kind could by themselves continue to reap the fruit which those of the Society are producing during their own lifetime."

With him Xavier took two Spanish Jesuits, Father Cosme de Torres and Brother Juan Fernandez, as well as an Indian and the three Japanese converts. The group first headed for Malacca, where after some time they found a Chinese junk to take them on to Japan. The two-month journey proved unpleasant, with rough seas and coarse company. The captain was nicknamed "the Thief," and the crew's rites to their sea god made Xavier uncomfortable. It was with much relief then that the mission landed at Yajiro's hometown of Kagoshima in southern Kyushu. It was August 15, 1549. Christianity had arrived in Japan.

Landings

The modern-day jetfoil from Tanegashima to Kagoshima runs a similar course to that of Xavier's junk, with the first part leading across choppy seas to Cape Sata on the southernmost tip of Kyushu (made famous through Alan Booth's book about walking the length of Japan). Once around the headland, there are calmer waters as the ship passes the picture-perfect Mt. Kaimon, known as the "Satsuma Fuji" for its conical shape (Satsuma was the local fiefdom). The boat then enters the expansive Kinko Bay, which extends inland for twenty-five miles. Lined with rocky sides and wooded hills, it makes for a welcoming backdrop to the country with its view of distant peaks: even the ugly blemishes of the twentieth century—factories, pylons and resort hotels—fail to mar the majesty.

Along the shoreline little fishing boats bob up and down, much as they would have done in Xavier's time, until one draws near the volcanic island of Sakurajima. Just over 3,600 feet in height, the mountain has erupted twenty-seven times since 1468, destroying whole villages and welding the island to an adjoining peninsula. A major eruption in 1914 left gray lava fields and a torii buried up to its neck. The volcano still remains active, and the city of Kagoshima on the opposite shore gets covered in an occasional film of ash. The day I arrived the fumes issuing from the barren peak were colored by the sunset to form an orange dragon's tail twisting dramatically up into the sky. Xavier and his fellow missionaries must have been impressed too by the dramatic beauty of the unknown land.

Since the jetfoil docks close to where the first mission landed, I took a taxi straight there and on the way asked the driver if the volcano was always so active. "Recently it's been rumbling a lot," the driver replied. "It's probably going to erupt soon, but don't worry. It won't happen today." At the landing site, a relief sculpted by a Belgian artist shows Xavier being carried ashore from a junk while a group of locals, including a two-sworded samurai, look on curiously. It's not hard to imagine the interest the multiracial group must have aroused. Along with the robed Europeans were the Indian, a Eurasian, a Chinese servant and the three foreign-speaking Japanese, no doubt with crosses around their necks.

As I stood in the park by the water's edge, I noticed with surprise the peak of Mt. Takachiho in the distance. According to Shinto myth, the mountain is the place where a grandson of Amaterasu, the sun goddess, "descended from Heaven." How extraordinary that the arrival of Xavier should have happened within sight of the mythic mountain. Could it be just by chance that these two very different "landings" had taken place so close to each other? Or was it rather a matter of geography, as in Tanegashima, with the flow of ocean currents bringing immigrants to the same welcoming bay? Coincidence or not, it made for a curious paradox. One religion was tribal in essence, based on particularism. The other originated in the Middle East and claimed to be universal. Japan was a land of gods, but Xavier and his companions had arrived to make it a land of God. What a challenge!

It must have been bizarre, this first encounter. A painting by the modern artist Seiji Utsumi shows European giants in black robes and wide-brimmed hats towering over a crowd of curious Japanese in loose clothing and straw sandals. The customs and behavior were unlike anything the Westerners had encountered before: the bowing and kneeling, the nodding and manner of conversation. Men had shaved foreheads, wore kimonos and carried fans, while the women had blackened teeth and shaved eyebrows. Some of the local priests dressed in black robes, while others wore white and had tall hats. The porters were virtually naked, and sexes bathed together unashamedly. Houses were made of wood and had paper screens for windows. Writing was from top right to bottom left. Every country is different, it has been said, but Japan is more different than any other. How much truer that would have been in the past!

The peculiarities of Japan as seen through European eyes were later spelled out in a list of 611 items by a Jesuit priest called Luis Frois (1532–97). His *Tratado* (1585), translated as *Topsy-Turvy* by Robin Gill, was written to help Europeans understand the country. Some of the observations are timeless. Physical attributes, for instance: "Our noses are high, some aquiline; theirs are low with small nostrils." Other entries are clearly obsolete: "European women do all they can to whiten their teeth; Japanese use iron and vinegar to make their mouth and teeth black." In putting together his paired contrasts, Frois cast interesting light on the clash of cultures.

> In Europe, clarity of language is sought and ambiguity avoided. In Japan ambiguous words are good language and held in high estimate.
>
> We ask one omnipotent God for favors in this life and the other. The Japanese ask *kami* for temporal good, and *hotoke* [buddhas] for salvation.
>
> Among us, someone who changes faith is considered a traitor and an apostate. In Japan, one may change sect as often as one likes without infamy.
>
> Among us, killing oneself is considered a grave sin. The Japanese in war, when they can do no more, cut their belly to show their guts.
>
> With us there is no crucifixion; in Japan, it is something very common.
>
> We are passionate with anger running free and impatience barely tamed at all. They, in some strange manner, control themselves and thus are moderate and prudent.

> With us, men join religious orders to make peni-
> tence and save themselves; the bonzes [Buddhist
> priests] enter religious orders to live in idleness and
> luxury and escape work.
>
> We drink with one hand; they always drink with
> two. We drink seated on a chair; they, sitting on their
> knees. With us, no one drinks more than he himself
> wants to . . . Japanese are so demanding they make
> some throw up and others drunk. Among us, mak-
> ing loud noises while we eat or gulping down wine
> is considered gross; the Japanese think they are both
> just dandy.

The differences were at their starkest in terms of hygiene, for the Europeans were unfussed about cleanliness whereas the Japanese were meticulous. The notion that bathing was unnatural and unhygienic was so prevalent in Europe that according to Bill Bryson's *At Home*, "By the eighteenth century the most reliable way to get a bath was to be insane." It doesn't take much imagination to realize how after months at sea the unwashed sailors must have struck the Japanese as hairy barbarians indeed. Eating with their hands and blowing their noses on their sleeves, the newcomers not only looked uncouth but were said to give off an unpleasant odor due to the dairy products they ate. By contrast, the Europeans were staggered to find Japanese bathed not just every day, but sometimes even twice a day. The immersion in hot water was too indulgent for the Jesuits, so they compromised by allowing themselves a bath once a week in summer and fortnightly in winter. If cleanliness is next to godliness, there's no doubting that spiritually the Japanese were on a higher plane.

First footsteps

The morning after my arrival in Kagoshima I headed for Xavier Church, where I was to meet up with a volunteer guide called Matsumoto-san. A Buddhist all his life, he'd married a Christian as a young man and his wife had brought up their daughters in her own faith. Now, in his retirement, he'd decided to join the rest of his family, and two years previously had converted to Catholicism. I gathered that companionship rather than faith was the motivation: no doubt, like my Japanese partner, he thought one *kami* as good as another. We went first to the park in front of the church, or rather the patch of bare earth with swings that often passes for a park in Japan. In one of the corners stood three statues put up in 1999 to mark the 450th anniversary of the arrival of Christianity, and the choice of figures was interesting. As well as Xavier and Yajiro, there was the less well-known Bernardo.

In a sense, Bernardo represents the counterpart of the Tanegashima Portuguese, for he is the first Japanese known to have reached Europe. One of Xavier's earliest converts, he became a devoted disciple and left Japan with the missionary in 1551 bound for Goa. From there he sailed for Lisbon, arriving in 1553. Xavier intended for him "to see the Christian religion in all its majesty" so that he could impress his fellow countrymen on his return. While in Portugal, Bernardo joined the Jesuits and studied at the College of Coimbra before traveling to Rome, where he met with Ignatius de Loyola and the pope. He apparently died of a fever in Portugal in 1557, but sadly this cultural pioneer left behind no account of his impressions. What did he make of the peculiarities of Europe, with its odd customs and topsy-turvy culture?

Xavier Church is a striking modern building, sadly strangled by telephone wires and hemmed in by ugly apartments. Built to commemorate Xavier's landing, it has a ship-like shape, at the front of which is a narrow bell tower that rises like a mast. Halfway up the stairs I noticed a relief showing the arrival of the first mission, with Yajiro and his two companions at the prow of the junk peering towards their hometown. Behind them stand the Europeans, and at the back the Indian convert and a caricature Chinese with exaggeratedly slanted eyes. The two Asians are usually written out of accounts, and while it was good to see them given recognition, one could have wished for greater sensitivity. When I pointed this out to Matsumoto, he was at pains to tell me how international the church was. "We have two Japanese priests, one Filipino and one Vietnamese," he said. Since I didn't respond, he repeated the information as if to impress on me how very singular it was. Immersed in the intercultural world of Xavier, I'd quite forgotten the insularity of provincial Japan and how exotic foreigners remain, even today.

Inside the church, an orchestra and twenty-voice choir were rehearsing for a concert, flooding the building with joyous sounds. The musicians looked at home, for the hexagonal room resembles a recital hall as much as a place of worship. The stained-glass windows are divided into monochrome sections, with red symbolizing, in the words of a pamphlet, "Xavier's passion for this mission and also the color of martyr's blood." Afterwards, in the vestibule I noticed a picture of Xavier's mummified corpse in Goa, and more macabrely, a picture of his severed right arm. It had been cut off at the elbow in 1614 and sent to Rome to prove the "miraculous preservation" of his body. In 1999, bizarrely, it made a tour of Japan. A severed right arm might seem the stuff of horror movies, but for Catholics there must be a sense that something of Xavier lingers in the lifeless limb. It set me thinking about the relationship between spirit and body, for in Shinto objects such as a rock, a doll, a branch—a whole mountain, even—can act as a sacred "body" (*goshintai*) into which the *kami* descends. Not unlike the Catholic mass, in fact, when the holy spirit enters into the communion wafers. Physical matter and the mysterious spark of life: isn't that what underlies every religious impulse, regardless of the form it takes?

Language matters

From Xavier Church, Matsumoto-san took me to the ruined site of Fukushoji, a Zen monastery that once dominated the city. It had been among the country's three biggest monasteries, with up to a staggering 1,500 monks in training. The sprawling complex was destroyed in the anti-Buddhist movement of 1869, when the Meiji government pushed a Shinto agenda, after which a high school was built on the site. Now all that remains from the original is the large cemetery, which holds the graves of the Shimazu lords who ruled the domain. In the early days of the mission, Xavier had made friends with the fifteenth head of the monastery, the eighty-two-year-old Ninshitsu, though the missionary was puzzled by exactly what the prelate believed. "I have found him hesitant and unable to decide if our soul is immortal or if it dies together with the body," he wrote in a letter to Europe. He was intrigued too about the purpose of meditation, and by way of an answer received a typically Zen response: "Some of them are counting up how much they received during the past months . . . others about where they can obtain better clothes . . . others are thinking about their recreations and amusements: in short, none of them are thinking about anything that has any meaning at all."

This first interreligious friendship raises the question of language, for one can't help wondering how Xavier and his fellow Europeans would have communicated. "If we knew how to speak Japanese, I have no doubt in believing that many would become Christians," he wrote. "We are now like so many statues among them. We are learning the language like little children." It's a feeling with which all newcomers to Japan can sympathize. At first Yajiro and his two companions acted as translators, while the three Westerners set about studying. Forty days later, remarkably, Xavier was attempting to explain the Ten Commandments in Japanese. This was managed by reading out texts that had been transliterated by Yajiro into Roman letters. What the locals made of long-nosed strangers reciting in broken Japanese peculiar stories of faraway places can only be imagined. Unsurprisingly, converts were few and far between.

Much of the mission's message was lost in translation, including the most vital of all—God. This owed itself to a simple blunder by Yajiro, who came up with the nearest equivalent he could think of: a Buddhist deity called Dainichi. As a result people simply assumed the newcomers were preaching a new type of Buddhism. It was a reasonable assumption: after all, they had arrived from India where Buddhism originated, and the newcomers were openly referred to as *Tenjiku-jin* (People of the Heavenly Land, i.e. Indians). Their talk of Dainichi must have heartily confused the Japanese. Why did the Christ of whom they spoke not recognize the reality of rebirth? What were his views on karma? Which of the sutras was his favorite?

A further problem for the newcomers was that Dainichi was not a Creator in the Christian sense, but synonymous with the totality of existence: "Life force who illuminates the universe" is one description. In this sense, the deity is more pantheistic than transcendental, and the linguistic mismatch was compounded by a conceptual issue, for the idea of an all-mighty being who stood outside the confines of the world was unknown to the Japanese. (Endo Shusaku, author of *Silence*, claimed the whole idea of transcendence was alien to the Japanese mind-set and a major impediment to the spread of Christianity.) Church historians have tended to blame Yajiro for the misunderstandings, but his translation of "God" seems not unreasonable given that he was neither a linguist nor an intellectual. He was after all the first person in history to be confronted with the problem, and it is hardly surprising that he should have reached for the nearest equivalent.

It took almost two years for Xavier to realize the gravity of the problem. It happened in Yamaguchi while he was talking with priests from the Shingon sect of Buddhism, for whom Dainichi was the central deity. The Japanese were interested in learning more about Christianity, and in response to their questions he told them that the Dainichi of which he spoke had neither color nor shape, with no beginning or end. "Then we are both following the same law," they told him. It prompted the missionary to wonder whether it might be true. There were after all so many similarities—the chanting, the robes, the incense, the prayer beads, the monasteries, the meditation, the one Supreme Deity. Saint Thomas had spread Christianity to Asia, and there was a real possibility that an offshoot of some sort had reached Japan. Xavier remembered that Yajiro had told him once that paintings of Dainichi showed the deity with one body and three heads: could it be a reference to the Trinity? Excitedly, the missionary asked the priests if the second of the Dainichi triad had been crucified in a Middle Eastern country, but the suggestion was met with guffaws and bewilderment. The missionary quickly realized his mistake.

Previously, the Christians called on people to praise Dainichi; now Xavier gave instructions to preach that Dainichi was the devil! No doubt, the locals were greatly confused. No doubt too, the Buddhists were much offended. In place of Dainichi, the Jesuits tried Deus, which with a Japanese pronunciation came out as Deusu. It sounded dangerously close to *Daiuso*, meaning "Big Lie," and the notion of foreigners proclaiming a Big Lie in the Sky was too tempting for the wits of the day. Thereafter the Christians turned to safer terms such as Tenshuu (Lord of the Heavens), and efforts were made to strip their language of Buddhist terms.

In 1555, a Portuguese priest identified over fifty problematic words in the Japanese-language catechism being used by missionaries. These all carried a Buddhist connotation, meaning that the newcomers were seen as a heretical sect rather than an altogether different religion. Instead, it was decided to retain Latin or Portuguese words for new concepts, and instead of referring to themselves by the Japanese term for priest, they distinguished themselves from Buddhists by using the word *bateren* (from the Portuguese term, *padre*). From now on the literature was to be filled with the colorful language of *bateren* battling with Buddhist bonzes (from *bouzu*, the Japanese word for "priest").

Given all this, it's small wonder that the later mission was much concerned with language learning. Seminaries ran special courses, and along with religious texts the first Christian presses in Japan produced grammar books, readers and dictionaries. But this was well after Xavier's time, and the man from Navarre had to muddle along as best he could. Already past his prime, he struggled with Japanese and in a report to Rome wrote of it being "the devil's own tongue" designed to prevent the spreading of the gospel. Fortunately, his younger colleague, Brother Fernandez, only twenty-two when he came to Japan, was a quick learner and acted as mouthpiece for the group as they negotiated their way through the minefield of Japanese politics.

Hopes raised and dashed

From the ruins of Fukushoji, Matsumoto-san took me to two other sites associated with Xavier. We headed first for Ichiujijo, the castle where not long after his arrival he was granted an audience with the feudal lord, Shimazu Takahisa. Japan at this time was plunged in the midst of a volatile period known as the Age of Warring Factions, in which there was little if any central control. It meant that the autonomous domains were virtually independent, and the feudal lords, known as daimyo, were free to do as they liked. To the Jesuits they were "kings" of their own little countries. It turned out to be fortuitous for them, for should the door be shut in one domain the missionaries could knock on another.

The site of the Shimazu castle lies eleven miles outside Kagoshima, an easy walk for a missionary used to long distances. The lush forests and bamboo of Xavier's time are now interspersed with concrete-covered hillsides, long tunnels and a huge bridge spanning a tiny valley. Food chains such as Kentucky Fried Chicken and Joyfull Restaurant stand out among the anonymous buildings. Then all of a sudden came a large road sign saying PRESUMED GRAVE OF YAJIRO, and we pulled up on the crest of a hill before a small pile of stones. There was no sign of a cross, and no name either. "Maybe it is not really his grave," said Matsumoto. "Maybe it was just a legend from long ago."

It's uncertain in fact what happened to the convert in later years, and some reports even have him ending up a pirate. Either way he had a fascinating life, and one surely fit for a novel or film. A fugitive from justice, he had traveled as far as India and served as the first cultural informant of his country to the Europeans. The welcome extended to the mission was of his making, and he made several converts himself among family and friends. In a letter to Goa he noted that his countrymen were "happy to hear me when I speak to them about the things of Jesus Christ. Even the priests are not offended: on the contrary they are much pleased when I speak of the law of the Christians." It shows the general open-mindedness in terms of religion.

It was thanks to Yajiro that Xavier managed to obtain an audience with the all-powerful daimyo. The castle where they met was abandoned not long afterwards, and there is little left now but rising slopes and stone remnants. Oddly, there is a statue of Xavier but none of his host, which struck me as an instance of Japanese largesse to an honorable visitor. In the missionary's time, there were houses within the outer earthen walls, and he would have climbed up past them to the prince's palace at the top, marked now by a stone cross. Xavier was forty-three, Takahisa thirty-five. What on earth did they make of each other? Despite the gulf in backgrounds, reports suggest that they got on well. The educated Takahisa, well-versed in Buddhist scripture, was not only curious about the new religion but eager for good relations with the Europeans because of the trade possibilities.

From Takahisa's castle with its commanding views, we drove to the more modest hill of Tsurumaru Castle where a samurai vassal of Takahisa lived. It was here that Xavier had his greatest success in the region, thanks to the administrator of the small castle known by his baptised name of Miguel. He had invited the European after hearing him preach in Kagoshima, and Xavier was able to make many conversions during his visit. They included the samurai's wife and retainers. He himself refrained from converting out of apprehension for what his daimyo might think. Before departing, Xavier was asked for a method of healing (Japanese were used to getting "worldly benefits" from their religion), and he left Miguel with a scourge, telling him to cure the sick by applying five mild blows to the infected area while invoking Jesus and Mary. Catholic superstition had entered rural Japan.

The success of his outing to Tsurumaru raised Xavier's hopes, but ten months into the mission disaster struck, when all at once Takahisa turned against the newcomers and forbade further conversions on the pain of death. For some time, Buddhist priests had been lobbying against the Christians, antagonized by the criticism of their behavior and beliefs. Matters came to a head when it was learned that a Portuguese ship had landed at Hirado in the north of Kyushu, for it meant that Takahisa's patronage of the Christians had failed to win him the trade he desired. In his vexation he banned further proselytizing. The mission had stalled, with just one hundred converts.

With no further prospects in Kagoshima, Xavier traveled by boat to Hirado, where he was given a fine welcome by the captain who had the cannon fired in salute. This impressed the local daimyo, who gave the missionary a warm welcome and granted him a license to preach. Within a short time, he had managed another hundred converts. Xavier was eager to move on, however, for he had already formulated a plan to visit "the king of Japan" in his capital at Kyoto (known at the time as Miyako). His intention was to secure permission for a church there as well as a Portuguese trading post at Sakai on the coast (now part of Osaka). At the same time he hoped to engage the country's leading Buddhists in debate, for he had heard of the city's famed "university" on Mt. Hiei. Trained in logic at Paris, he was confident of being able to defeat his opponents and win the favor of Japan's top rulers. The next chapter of his journey was to take him to the very heart of the country, where no European had ever been before. In his quest to spread Christianity, the missionary was proving to be an intrepid and pioneering explorer.

Chapter Two

The Word
(Yamaguchi)

Disappointment

In late 1550 Xavier set off on the first stage of his journey to Kyoto, making his way to the regional capital of Yamaguchi in eastern Honshu. At the time it was a flourishing city, second in the country in terms of importance. Known as the "Kyoto of the West," it had been modeled on the nation's capital when it was established in the fourteenth century. Now, paradoxically, it's the country's smallest prefectural capital, but you get a feel of the former glory from buildings like the five-story Rurikoji. It must have impressed Xavier when he visited.

In the bustling midst of Yamaguchi, the small band of intrepid Christians set about preaching in the streets. They added an exotic touch to an already colorful scene as Brother Fernandez read out passages explaining the story of Creation, while Xavier prayed silently alongside. The Japanese had three great sins, the foreigners declared: idolatry, sodomy and infanticide (the latter was practiced by the poor to control numbers). The spectacle drew a crowd of onlookers, and while some listened politely others openly laughed or became angry. One man even spat in the face of the younger Jesuit. Yet the newcomers aroused interest, and they received invitations to the houses of noblemen, curious to hear more of the new religion. The connections enabled them to obtain an audience with the local daimyo, Ouchi Yoshitaka (1507–51).

Yoshitaka was a cultured intellectual with an interest in Confucianism, and he listened to the missionaries politely before all of a sudden walking out and bringing the audience to an end. It came just after a denunciation of sodomy, leading commentators to suppose that Yoshitaka himself indulged in a practice that was widespread among samurai. The sexual bond between older warrior and young apprentice, known as *shudo*, was such an accepted part of Japanese culture that some have compared it to "boy worship" in ancient Greece. On this point there could be no meeting of minds with the missionaries.

Despite the setback, Xavier continued with his plan to head for Kyoto, taking with him Bernardo and Brother Fernandez. Over 70 percent of Japan is mountainous, and since ancient times much of the travel has been by water. Coastal villages often had more interaction with each other than with neighbors in the next valley. Accordingly, Xavier and his companions set off from Yamaguchi for the Inland Sea, from where they took a boat to Sakai, the port serving the capital. It was no easy journey, undertaken in midwinter with the two Europeans sharing just a single blanket. For those of us used to creature comforts, the very thought is horrendous. Swollen feet, pirates and being stoned by village children were just some of the problems the group encountered.

In Sakai, they were able to stay with a rich merchant with connections in Kyoto. When I visited the city, I discovered to my surprise that it still celebrates the missionary's brief stay, and not far from the railway station is a park dedicated to his memory. Keen to exploit its past, modern Sakai makes much of its ties with the Portuguese, and I found myself, to my bemusement, riding a "Nambanjin bus" to the park decorated with pictures of oversized Southern Barbarians from the sixteenth century. A signboard in the park states grandiosely that: ON A CERTAIN DAY IN 1550 SAINT FRANCIS XAVIER LANDED HERE AT SAKAI AND BECAME A GUEST IN THE MANSION OF RYOKEI HIBIYA. FROM THIS MEMORABLE DAY DATES THE ADVENT OF OCCIDENTAL CIVILIZATION IN JAPAN WHICH ADDED MUCH TO THE FRAGRANCE OF THE MODERN CULTURE.

From Sakai the missionary group joined a procession headed for the capital, walking two days across snow-covered hills and sleeping in the mountains like *yamabushi* ascetics. It was mid-January 1551 when they arrived in Kyoto, but to their dismay they found it largely in ruins after civil war and long years of neglect. Where once had stood grand buildings were fields of grass. Through their Sakai contact they were able to stay in the house of a merchant in the city center, from where they walked four hours around to Sakamoto at the base of Mt. Hiei. Their goal was Enryaku-ji, one of the largest temple complexes in the world, with five hundred buildings scattered through sixteen valleys. Yet though the Jesuits tried hard to see the head priests, it was made plain to them that there could be no access without precious gifts to smooth the way.

The missionaries had little success elsewhere in Kyoto. The "king of Japan" whom Xavier hoped to see was a shogun in exile from his own capital. In his absence, the group turned their attention to the emperor, who had symbolic significance but no actual power. Because of the conditions in the country, the revenue of the imperial household had dried up, and the emperors of the age were so impoverished that one had to resort to selling calligraphy like a street artist, while another was unable for years to afford his inauguration ceremony. Again it was made clear to the small band that their shabby appearance and lack of customary gifts meant there was no chance of an audience. Though they tried preaching in the streets, people were preoccupied with a possible outbreak of hostilities. "When we saw that the land did not have the peace there for preaching the law of God, we returned," Xavier reported. The visit had proved a total failure: it lasted just eleven days.

A second attempt

Despite the setback, Xavier had learned some important lessons, not the least of which was the significance of regional lords in the absence of central rule. At the time none had higher prestige than the daimyo of Yamaguchi, so Xavier decided to try again at winning his favor. The second meeting was a complete contrast to the first. Rather than an impoverished missionary, the European now appeared as the dignified envoy of a foreign power, complete with official letters from the governor of Goa. Instead of a well-worn robe, he dressed in a splendid silk cassock brought from Hirado and carried gifts designed to impress. These included brocades, textiles, cut glass, a table service, Portuguese wine, a pair of spectacles and a telescope. Of particular fascination to the Japanese, who were still using sundials, was a mechanical clock. And in addition to all this the modern-day saint was able to offer the daimyo an elaborately carved three-barrel musket.

The result this time was a definite success. Yoshitaka not only granted the priests a license to preach but gave them premises in an abandoned temple called Daidoji. For four months Xavier lived and preached there, a time that he found highly rewarding. "I think I could truly say that in my life I have never received so much joy and spiritual satisfaction," he wrote. People flocked to the temple to hear the twice-daily talks, with samurai and noblemen staying to engage in discussion afterwards. Why did God create evil and suffering if he was all-mighty? Why should it be impossible to get out of hell once consigned there? And why should ancestors be sent there if they had never had the chance to learn of Christianity? The questions ranged beyond religion to matters of geography and science, which the Paris scholar was able to handle adroitly. He was in his element, and the harvest in this short period was some five hundred converts (one of whom, a blind *biwa* player named Lorenzo, was to play a key role in the Kyoto mission).

There's a park in modern Yamaguchi that marks the site of these events. The location was lost during Edo times, when Christianity was in disfavor, but a sliding screen was found in the mid-nineteenth century with a painting of the city in its prime, which enabled rough identification of where Daidoji stood. Now a simple memorial commemorates the site where the new-comers set up base (it later became the country's first ever church). The town boasts too a Xavier Memorial Church, rebuilt in 1998 after a mysterious fire destroyed its predecessor. The original was in a Romanesque style that echoed the facade of Xavier Castle in Navarre. The present church by contrast is a striking modern design, triangular in shape to suggest "the tent of God." There's a small exhibition, with stained glass that tells the story of the missionary's life, up to his fond farewell with the Yamaguchi faithful.

When Xavier heard that a Portuguese ship had landed in the domain of Bungo in the east of Kyushu, the missionary hurried to get news, for he was still nominally in charge of affairs at Goa. He found there was no correspondence for him, however, and as a consequence felt compelled to travel back with the ship. During his short stay in Bungo, he met with Mendes Pinto, the merchant who claimed to have landed at Tanegashima. After fourteen years in the Far East, the Portuguese adventurer had become wealthy, and he gave the mission a substantial sum for the building of a church in Yamaguchi. Xavier was also able to win an audience with the Bungo daimyo, Otomo Sorin, despite the alarming pic-ture given of the missionary by Buddhist priests: "They say they have seen him at different times talking to demons with whom he has dealings and that he uses sorcery to trick the ignorant and gullible. They also say he is not just poor, but so poor that even the lice crawling over his body are so sickened that they will not taste his flesh."

Xavier was defended from these charges by the captain of the Portuguese carrack, who argued that, despite appearances, the priest could commandeer a European ship any time he wanted and was in fact a powerful man with high status. It opened the way to an audience with the daimyo, who subsequently donated a building to the Jesuits that became their headquarters. Twenty-seven years later when he converted to Christianity, he took the name of Francisco in honor of the missionary.

After two and a quarter years in Japan, Xavier departed Japan leaving behind some one thousand converts. It was a toehold from which he hoped that others could advance. He himself had every intention of returning, and in a letter to Ignatius Loyola he wrote that "Japan is the only country yet discovered in these regions where there is hope of Christianity permanently taking root." He was also motivated to develop work in China, since he noted the readiness of Japanese to emulate the culture there. After returning to Goa, however, he died the next year from disease on a small Chinese island while on the way to intercede with the emperor on behalf of Portuguese prisoners. In 1622 he was canonized by the Catholic Church and today is known as the patron saint of missionaries.

Xavier's legacy was to shape the Japan mission. He was so impressed by the civilized nature of the Japanese that he called for only missionaries of the highest quality to be sent. Aware that the Portuguese tendency to look down on non-Europeans had an adverse effect, he made efforts to adapt to local ways and be culturally sensitive. He cut down on the consumption of meat, for example, for the Japanese ate little in accord with Buddhist precepts. These were applied for the most part to four-legged animals such as cows and horses, for fish and birds were part of the normal diet (also rabbits, which through a curious quirk were counted as birds since the verb for "fly"—*tobu*—also means "hop" or "jump").

When it came to Christian matters, however, Xavier showed little willingness to compromise. Like others of his age, he viewed any non-Catholic religion as the devil's means of distracting attention from the one true faith. In his rejection of Japanese religions, the missionary was absolute. Buddhist priests were vilified for corruption and laziness; Shinto animism with its worship of natural phenomena was dismissed as childish. By contrast, Japanese had long practiced *ta no wa* (harmony of diversity), and it had even been written into the country's first constitution in 604. Shinto and Buddhism were welded into a syncretic blend named *shin-butsu shugo*, which mixed *kami* and buddha worship. Elements of Taoism and Confucianism had also been integrated into this religious framework, and no doubt Christianity could have been absorbed too if its proselytizers had so wished. In rejecting Japanese religions, Xavier was in a sense rejecting Japanese tradition.

The first hidden Christian

Following Xavier's departure, Father Cosme de Torres (d. 1570) took over the running of the mission. The Spaniard is not very well known, but I find him an intriguing figure because of his adventurous background. He started out as a homegrown teacher until the lure of foreign parts took him to Mexico. He worked for four years in the capital before heading for the west coast, from where he took a ship for the brave new world opening up in Asia. He joined the Jesuits after meeting Xavier, to whom he became a trusted right-hand man in Goa, and when the idea of a mission to Japan came up he was ready to take it on. Though not as quick at learning Japanese as Brother Fernandez, he wrote the first explication of the country's religion in a report to Rome that even after five hundred years makes good sense. "They regard honor as their principle god," he noted. Such was his admiration for the people that the comments must have raised eyebrows among readers back in Europe: "If I should strive to write all the good qualities and virtues which are found in them, I should run out of paper and ink," he observed. That the Japanese should be so virtuous without having a belief in God is something on which he doesn't dwell, but it should surely have given him pause for thought.

Torres made history in Yamaguchi by celebrating Christmas in 1552 with a solemn High Mass, together with Brother Fernandez and a new arrival. Japanese converts were invited, and hymns were sung. Now the city is keen to exploit it as the country's first "Kurismasu," and it puts together an annual program to promote "Yamaguchi City, the birthplace of the Japanese Christmas." I came across a schedule for the 2010 celebrations and was amazed to find there were forty separate events, beginning—horrendously—as early as October 27. Hot spring concerts, a light-up of the river, and a shopping arcade party were some of the delights on offer. Xavier got his face on the pamphlet, together with Ouchi, but not, sadly, Torres.

Besides the first celebration of Christmas, the Spaniard was also to become the country's first hidden Christian in an episode that illustrates the extent to which the fortunes of the mission depended on the patronage of feudal lords. Shortly after Xavier's departure, the daimyo of Yamaguchi was overthrown in a rebellion, and the house where Torres and Brother Fernandez were living was sacked by men with spears who yelled "Tenjikujin" ("Indians") at them. "Let's kill them because they spoke evil of the *kami* and caused the outbreak of fighting," said the intruders, and the two Jesuits were lucky to escape with their lives. In a message smuggled out to Xavier, Torres said he was ready to preach Christianity in secret if need be—an indicator of how things would develop.

Torres returned to Yamaguchi after the uprising died down and was able to make use of Pinto's money to build the country's first church. In 1556 further disruption took place, however, when an avowed enemy of the Christians took power in Yamaguchi and destroyed the mission. By this time Torres had managed some two thousand converts, including noblemen, who were forced to flee the domain. Five years later a similar anti-Christian outburst took place in Hirado when the daimyo there, piqued at a Portuguese ship not choosing his port, forced believers to abjure their faith. According to a Jesuit report, some preferred to abandon all their possessions and move to Bungo, "poor with Christ rather than rich without him." It's said too that at this time the first martyrdom in Japan took place, when an unknown woman was beheaded for praying before a cross.

Like Xavier, Torres wrote that his time in Yamaguchi had been one of joy and satisfaction. He was heartbroken at the destruction of the mission there, but continued working optimistically until he died. According to the Church historian Luis Frois, "his modesty and religious maturity suited the nature of the Japanese so much that he won profound love and respect from them." Such was their attachment that some of the converts kept locks of his hair or pieces of his clothing. He had a particular interest in education and organized classes for children at which they not only studied Japanese but learned prayers in Latin. Modern Japan has many Christian educational institutions; here was their progenitor.

Kirishitan daimyo

The isolation of the Christian groups made conversion an uphill task, and ten years after the start of the mission there were just six thousand converts and six missionaries in the whole country. It seemed the faith was doomed to be a minor sect, hardly worth a mention in historical terms. Some of the religious concepts had proved so baffling to Japanese that they had trouble getting their minds around the new ideas. The notion of an eternal soul, for instance. Among the most common questions were inquiries about its color and shape. And since it was apparently free of rebirth, how did it differ from a *kami* or buddha? The concept of eternal hell also proved problematic, for in Buddhism there was always the possibility of rebirth into a better life. In a culture of ancestor worship, the idea that family members might have been consigned to everlasting damnation was devastating. "I can hardly restrain my tears sometimes," Xavier wrote, "at seeing men so dear to my heart suffer such immense pain about a thing that is already done with and can never be undone."

In 1563 the mission had a major breakthrough with the conversion of a daimyo in western Kyushu. Omura Sumitada (1533–87) was baptised following a promise by the Jesuits to bring Portuguese ships to his harbor, which enabled him to obtain guns and cannon to help secure his domain. Other daimyo were to follow suit, and between 1563 and 1620 a total of eighty-two in all were baptised (several were fathers and sons, and in at least one instance there were three generations of the same family). How far these daimyo were motivated by faith and how much by political advantage has been a matter of much debate, but there's little doubt that the ability of Jesuits to affect trade decisions was for many a determining factor. Otomo Sorin, for example, the Bungo daimyo who met with Xavier, wrote in a letter to the Jesuits that "My desire to win a victory over the land of

Yamaguchi is due to my wish to help the *Bateren* to return there and to give them more protection than before." Cunning words! They were designed to help get him saltpeter (an ingredient of gunpowder). It's been said that whereas the missionaries used trade to get the Japanese to heaven, the Japanese used heaven as a way to get trade. From the very outset, the fate of the mission was tied to a masthead.

In terms of trade the missionaries were greatly helped by the poor state of Sino-Japanese relations. For centuries the coasts of China had been plundered by smuggler-pirates known as *wako*, who were predominately Japanese. As a result, the country had broken off trade with Japan altogether, which enabled the Portuguese to fill the gap. Fine quality Chinese silk was ferried from Macao, together with textiles, gold, porcelain, musk, rouge, pepper, cloves and even—remarkably—hippopotamus tusk for *hanko* seals. European and Indian products were shipped too, particularly guns together with the saltpeter and lead they required, as well as furniture and exotic animals. Goods carried back on the reverse journey included copper, sulfur and Japanese handicrafts, though the chief item was silver, which was the means of payment to the Portuguese merchants. Such large quantities were transported that the vessel became known in Macao simply as the "Silver Ship."

Between 1549 and 1639 fifty-four Great Ships called at ports in Kyushu, mostly Hirado in the northwest and Nagasaki. The visit of a Portuguese carrack was a grand occasion, something akin in modern times to the arrival of a cruiser like the Queen Elizabeth in a Third World harbor. With four decks, the European ships were two or three times larger than an Asian junk. To ordinary Japanese they were known as *kurofune* (black ships), because during the two-year voyage from Europe the oil secreted by the pinewood would turn them black. The cargo of such a vessel meant a huge influx of revenue to the local port, so it was welcomed with fanfares and festivities. Portuguese sailors would line up on shore in all their finery as the captains proceeded to the residence of the local daimyo, accompanied by armed guard and cannon salutes. There he would be received as an important dignitary, with great pomp and elaborate feasts. For months on end the ship would rest at anchor as business was done with local merchants, and the bartering included more than just goods, as an Italian visitor, Francesco Carletti, noted (translated by Michael Cooper in the wonderful *They Came to Japan*):

> As soon as ever these Portuguese arrive and disembark, the pimps who control the traffic in women call on them in the houses in which they are quartered, and inquire whether they would like to purchase, or acquire in any other method they please, a girl for the period of their sojourn or to keep her for some many months, or for the night, or for a day, or for an hour. . . . To sum up, the country is more plentifully supplied than any other with these sort of means of gratifying the passion for sexual indulgence, just as it abounds in every other sort of vice, in which it surpasses every other place in the world.

The significance of the Christian daimyo extended beyond simple patronage, for the nature of Japanese feudalism meant that conversion would involve all their retinue and followers. "The daimyo make the best apostles," noted one Jesuit drily. Sometimes it went even further, for a daimyo might force conversion on the whole domain, involving tens of thousands of villagers. As a result, the number of baptisms leapt upwards, though the quality of converts was often unmatched by the quantity. Despite the best efforts of the priests, many of these new "Christians" were unaware even of the most fundamental tenets.

The shallowness of belief provoked a "breadth-versus-depth" debate among Jesuits. Was it better to have as many converts as possible, or was it better to have fewer but of firm faith? Those who favored breadth argued that baptism enabled salvation and that deeper understanding would follow later. Better to save souls while one could, ran the thinking, particularly as the mission needed funds and support. Those on the other side stressed the impossibility of Christianity taking root without proper understanding: a distorted faith was as bad as a false faith. The paucity of priests played a role in the debate too. In one instance, 35,000 converts were being taken care of by a single missionary who didn't speak Japanese, aided only by two native catechists (*dojuku*). Quite a workload!

In the end "breadth" defeated "depth," and emphasis was put on as rapid a growth as possible. Numbers were the name of the game, and it seemed the Jesuits were on a winning streak. The hundreds of baptisms at Yamaguchi turned into thousands all across Kyushu, and by 1579 the number of Japanese Christians amounted to almost 100,000. It was a tiny proportion of a population of over 20 million, but in the process the mission had won the favor of some of the highest in the land. With the ascendancy of the first great unifier of Japan, Oda Nobunaga, they even gained the goodwill of the most powerful man of the age. For the Church, as for the country as a whole, it marked a whole new era.

Chapter Three

Good News
(Azuchi)

King of Japan

The Jesuit strategy of seeking favor at the top found its greatest
reward at the time of Oda Nobunaga (1534–82), a colossus who
strides imperiously through the history of these times, dripping
blood as he goes. The first to unify Japan after a century of civil
strife, he rose to prominence from an obscure province in the
Nagoya region by beating a series of rivals. In 1568 he marched
into Kyoto, where he set about establishing his power in draconian fashion: "Govern the empire by military force," was his
maxim. Public opinion polls regularly cite him as the most influential Japanese of all time, revered as a Napoleonic hero of the
nation-state, yet for the historian George Sansom he was "a cruel
and callous brute." When I ask Japanese friends what they think
of him, they say *kowai* (frightening). He killed his own brother,
ordered the wholesale slaughter of opponents, and in his most vicious action laid waste the temple complex of Mt. Hiei, in which
an estimated 25,000 men, women and children were killed and
over 700 years of Buddhist culture literally went up in smoke.

Yet, like many a strongman, Nobunaga was also a man of cultured tastes, and along with the brutality went courage, intelligence and skill. He enjoyed the company of foreign missionaries,

one of whom was Luis Frois (1532–97), author of *Topsy-Turvy*. Their paths had first crossed when, as secretary to the Jesuit Superior, Frois had gone to visit Kyoto and been given a personal tour by Nobunaga of his new castle. He was invited too to stay at the warlord's private residence in Gifu, where he was able to observe his host at close quarters:

> The king of Owari would be about 37 years old, tall, thin, sparsely bearded, extremely warlike and much given to military exercises, inclined to works of justice and mercy, sensitive about his honor, reticent about his plans, an expert in military strategy, unwilling to receive advice from subordinates, highly esteemed and venerated by everyone, does not drink wine and rarely offers it to others, brusque in his manner, despises all the other Japanese kings and princes and speaks to them over his shoulder in a loud voice as if they were lowly servants, obeyed by all as the absolute lord, has good understanding and good judgment. He despises the *kami* and *hotoke* [buddhas] and all other pagan superstitions. Nominally belonging to the Hokke sect, he openly denies the existence of a creator of the universe, the immortality of the soul and life after death.

Following his entry into Kyoto, Nobunaga made a decisive intervention on behalf of the Christians. The small mission there had only been set up nine years earlier, but it had managed to have an impact on the samurai class, which aroused the hostility of influential Buddhists. As a result, the emperor was persuaded to issue an edict expelling the Christians, but Nobunaga rescinded the order and arranged for a debate. On one side stood Frois and the blind *biwa* musician, Lorenzo; on the other were the Buddhists, led by an anti-Christian named Nichijo Shonin. Frois has left a first-hand account, which reveals the almost comical gulf in understanding. "Whom do you worship?" demanded the Buddhist. "God, three in one, creator of heaven and earth," came the answer. "Show him to us," Nichijo demanded. When the Jesuits explained that he was invisible and eternal, the Buddhist burst out in exasperation that "All this is incomprehensible" and demanded they be exiled for deception. Things were shortly to get worse.

Irritated by the sophistry of the Jesuits, Nichijo snorted with derision at the idea of an immortal soul and again demanded they show him proof of its existence. Frois replied that it could only be seen with the inner eye. When people grow sick, he argued, they do not lose their mind; similarly when people die they do not lose their soul.

> At this the bonze rose up gnashing his teeth, and the color of his face changed in his rage and frenzy. "You say that the soul remains, but you must show it to me now," he shouted. "I'm going to cut off the head of your disciple here so that you can show me the substance that remains." He then rushed to grab a *naginata* [lance] and had to be restrained by Nobunaga and some of the lords in attendance.

Following the debate, Nobunaga extended his patronage to the Christians, and the friendly relations worked to the advantage of both sides. The warlord was canny enough to know that patronizing the missionaries would stand him in good stead with Portuguese traders, who delivered the guns and cannons he needed. His rule did not as yet extend outside the country's central regions, and there was still much fighting to be done. In the 1570s, for instance, he was troubled by the *ikko-ikki* religious uprisings, whose followers adhered to Jodo Shinshu (True Pure Land) beliefs. They had a virtually impregnable stronghold at their temple headquarters, Ishiyama Honganji (origin of modern-day Osaka), against which Nobunaga waged an eleven-year campaign. Eleven years! During the campaign a Christian general took up arms against him, and, concerned that a fellow convert would join the revolt, Nobunaga asked the Jesuits to intervene. In return he gave them permission to build a church and even dangled before them the possibility he might convert himself. He was as cunning off the battlefield as on it.

The austere lifestyle of the Jesuits seems to have impressed Nobunaga, who appreciated their commitment and vow of poverty. In his own circle there were practitioners of Zen whose martial discipline also accorded with the samurai values he espoused. Xavier's call for only the best of missionaries was paying dividends. By contrast, the warlord had a strong distaste for the hypocrisy of Buddhist priests (he confided to Frois that they disgusted him). As a long-established religion, Buddhism suffered from a similar malaise to pre-Reformation Catholicism, and Nobunaga was particularly irked by those who preached of suffering while living in luxury. Many of their temples were well-endowed, and some of the priests had a reputation for womanizing and drunkenness. Worst of all as far as Nobunaga was concerned, Buddhist sects had built up large militias of warrior-monks to protect their interests. Once in Kyoto, he showed his disdain for the religion by ordering the destruction of temples and statues to be used as building material for his new castle.

Nobunaga's feelings coincided with those of the Jesuits, for their belief in the one true faith led to some vicious attacks on Buddhist priests: "We hate and abominate the devil above all else," wrote Frois. "The bonzes venerate and worship him." No doubt such remarks were music to Nobunaga's ears. Rather than bridging the gap between the two faiths, the Jesuits constantly sought to exploit it. The similarity of the rosary to Buddhist prayer-beads was ascribed to a devilish attempt to confuse people, and the Amida sects with their promise of salvation through faith were written off as akin to the heresy of Martin Luther. Zen proved a tougher opponent, and in his *Historia* Frois relates how one of their number dropped in at the Kyoto church, where in conversation with Brother Lorenzo he was told of the glory of God and how trivial the power of *hotoke* (buddhas) were in comparison. The Zen priest responded with a dismissive laugh that such talk was childish and unworthy of wise men, for they lay in a realm beyond human knowledge. He had a point.

Azuchi: castle and seminary

The Azuchi era (1573–82) in which Nobunaga held power takes its name from the castle he built on the shores of Lake Biwa, and it's there that I headed to get a better understanding of the events of these years. The train drops one at a sleepy little town, more a village really, that makes you wonder if you've got off at the wrong stop. Could this really once have been the power base of the country? Yet as you emerge from the tiny station you're greeted by a large statue of Nobunaga, based on a portrait by the Jesuit painter Giovanni Niccolo, which is said to be the best surviving resemblance. It shows him with a surprisingly thick mustache, haughty nose and elongated face as if flattened on both sides. Instead of the ruthlessness I'd expected, there was an air of calm intelligence.

Half an hour's walk brings one to the almost 600-feet-high Azuchi Hill, on which the wily strongman chose to site his castle. It not only controlled trading routes but enabled him to keep an eye on his enemies in Kyoto while avoiding the city's frequent fires and intrigues. It took over three years before it was completed in 1579, and Frois thought it as grand a castle as any he'd seen in Europe. Though nothing remains now but the foundations, you get a feel for the former grandeur by the huge stone slabs and steep steps leading up the side of the hill. On the lower slopes lived Nobunaga's chief vassals. "Inside the walls are many beautiful and exquisite houses," wrote Frois, "all of them decorated with gold and so neat and well-fashioned that they seem to reach the acme of human elegance."

From the top there is a commanding view of the neighboring plain, while on the other side the hill overlooks an outlying part of Lake Biwa. I was surprised to find a formal grave for Nobunaga, since I'd previously visited two others for the warlord in Kyoto. The Japanese custom of *bunkotsu* (divided bones) can be disorienting for those who like to commune with the dead, since you can never be sure what, if anything, a grave contains. A signboard declared helpfully that in this case it contained his hat, kimono and sword. It was here too that the official Buddhist rites had taken place for him.

The castle's high point, literally, was a huge seven-story building that stood at the very top. It seemed to Frois to be reaching up to heaven, indicative of Nobunaga's high ambition. The bottom three floors were open-plan in the middle as if in imitation of tall-ceilinged European cathedrals, beneath which was a basement for arms storage. The top three floors were the most ostentatious, and there's a recreation of them at a nearby museum. They present a dazzling spectacle, with gilded surface and paintings that draw on Buddhist, Taoist and Confucian themes. The warlord wanted to incorporate the country's ideologies under one roof—his own roof! He even had himself deified at the specially built temple, Sokenji, to lend his rule the aura of divinity, and he issued a proclamation that threatened unbelievers with hell, not just in a future life but in this. "I therefore repeat," thundered the living god, "that it is essential that everybody should show the deepest reverence."

Around the castle a small town of five thousand people sprang up, and thanks to Nobunaga's patronage the missionaries were able to set up a school for the children of noblemen. The site lies across some rice fields from the castle hill and is marked by a stone sign saying SEMINARIO. The three-story Jesuit building that stood here had the same blue-colored tiles as the castle, indicative of the prestige the Christians enjoyed. Inside were living quarters for the priests, a large communal space, and a dormitory for thirty-three students. It was run by Father Organtino, in charge of the Kyoto mission, and the course of studies included Latin and the history of Christianity, as well as music and Japanese literature.

The Seminario proved a learning experience in more ways than one, for the experiment in cultural cohabitation was not without its frictions. Parents expected the seclusion of the young novices to be temporary, as with Buddhist practice, but for the Jesuits it was the beginning of a lifelong commitment. Although the rules of poverty forbade material possessions, for the Japanese gift giving was such an integral part of life that refusal was a great insult. Confession too was problematic in a culture that encouraged emotional suppression, and ancestor worship also proved a source of conflict, for the young seminarians were unable to take part in such vital family festivals as Obon.

Nobunaga once paid a surprise visit to the seminary, and was entertained by a recital of European music. "Of all the things introduced into Japan so far," ran a missionary report, "the playing of organs, harpsichords and viols please the Japanese most. After that he [Nobunaga] went to see the bell and other curious things which the Fathers kept in that house. Such things are very necessary to attract the pagans who flock to see them out of curiosity; we have learned from daily experience that these things act as a bait, because they help people to get to know us and to listen to our sermons." One sees here how the Jesuits lured people with appetizing "bait": fishers of men, indeed!

At the site of the Seminario there is now a small park, and as I sat on a bench looking towards the castle hill, I fell to wondering if Father Organtino had looked up from the same spot to give thanks to "his lord." My musings were interrupted when a villager walking his dog came up to ask in broken English where I was from. When I told him in Japanese I had come from Kyoto especially to see the Seminario, he was astonished. "It's a pity it was only used for three years," I said by way of conversation, "because it was destroyed when Nobunaga was killed, wasn't it?" I was hoping he might tell me some local lore, but in his amazement at a foreigner knowing such things he was rendered speechless. Back at the railway station I pondered whether Father Organtino too had encountered such reactions. One imagines curiosity about the Europeans was much stronger in those days, but perhaps ideas about "Japanese uniqueness" were not so prevalent. Certainly, however, there was a fascination with the exotic ways of the foreigners, for these years witnessed the beginnings of a peculiar *Namban* (Southern Barbarian) boom, which proved helpful to the Christian cause.

Favor and fashion

Under Nobunaga, the Christian cause progressed in leaps and bounds, helped by the favor that the leader showed towards the Europeans. According to George Sansom, "it became almost fashionable in some quarters to be baptised and carry a rosary." Society people even sported European clothing such as doublets, and there was great interest in the capes, frilled ruffs and ungainly baggy trousers worn to keep cool and ward off insect bites in hot climates. Food was introduced with a Portuguese touch, such as tempura and cakes with refined sugar. "*Namban* sauce" still remains popular today. There was even a genre of painting known as *Namban-ga*, which featured Westerners with long noses and strange habits. One of my favorites shows a priest in robes with exaggerated features, looking for all the world like a *tengu* monster preaching to a samurai. (There's a delicious irony in this, for Jesuits used the word *tengu* to signify Satan.)

These were good years for the mission: as Frois noted, more were being baptised in a single month than in the whole of the mission's first eighteen years put together! Such was the optimism that Father Organtino claimed that Japan would be Christian within thirty years if more priests were available. He had good grounds for the claim. Not only was Nobunaga happy to fraternize with Catholics—he met with the Jesuits on twenty-seven different occasions—but he was good friends with Father Organtino and visited the Namban-ji (Southern Barbarian Temple) in Kyoto. He even let his sons develop an interest in the religion: the oldest invited Organtino to start a mission at his residence in Gifu, and the second son was later baptised. (Referred to by the Jesuits as Gohonjo, he made an attempt to succeed his father and would have thus become a Christian shogun.)

In Kurosawa's film *Kagemusha* (*The Shadow Warrior,* 1980) Nobunaga appears in Western clothes, drinks red wine, and responds with "Amen" when blessed by a Catholic priest. It was all based on historical research. The warlord once went so far as to say to the Jesuits, "I swear to you . . . that there is no difference between my heart's feelings and the Padre's doctrine." It had taken some three hundred years to get the Roman emperor Constantine to proclaim Christianity a state religion, yet here the Jesuits were poised at the same point after just thirty. It was astonishing progress, and the mission seemed on the point of creating a Christian country in a part of the world that barely even flickered on the European consciousness.

So how close did Nobunaga come to converting? By all accounts, not close at all. Though he enjoyed the company of missionaries, with their advanced learning and tales of foreign countries, he was not concerned with their religion. Frois wrote as much in a letter to a fellow Jesuit: "His questions are largely about the state of affairs in Europe and India, and he shows not the slightest interest in the Word of Our Lord Jesus Christ." Matters of faith were of little consequence to the power-hungry potentate, and no doubt the calculating warlord was playing the Jesuits along for his own purposes. He saw them as useful for goading the Buddhists and beneficial for trade. Their religion he could take or leave.

As it happened, the most startling development of these years did not happen at Azuchi, but in distant Nagasaki, which was unexpectedly ceded to the Jesuits. The area had been virtually unknown until a priest named Luis de Almeida visited a small fishing village in 1567 and noted the potential for ships to anchor there. It lay in the domain of a Christian daimyo, with whom the missionaries wished the Portuguese to trade, and in 1572 came the first carrack. Within a short time the simple one-street village had expanded into a town of 25,000 as trade opportunities developed and Christians moved to escape persecution. Churches were built, Portuguese traders settled and the town took on a European flavor. Even the Japanese citizens ate beef and drank wine. The Japanese word for bread—*pan* (from the Portuguese)—originated here, and a type of cake called *kasutera* (Castille) is still sold in Nagasaki today.

In 1580 the daimyo of the area, Omura Sumitada, faced with hostile forces in surrounding territories, decided to cede administration of Nagasaki to the Jesuits in order to tie himself to powerful allies. He also ensured himself a refuge, should his domain be overrun. For their part the cash-strapped Jesuits gained a financial lifeline, for the expanding mission was in bad need of funds, and in subsequent years roughly half of their running costs were covered by Nagasaki's harbor fees and trade tariffs. In this way, just thirty years after Xavier, the mission had established a "Japanese Vatican" with a harbor that ranked alongside Goa, Malacca and Macao as a Portuguese haven. No longer were the Jesuits marginal to Japan, for they now had a stake in the affairs of the country. Armed with Portuguese guns and cannon, Nagasaki was a Jesuit stronghold in a very real sense.

From the early beginnings in Kagoshima, the mission had come a long way. Though small in terms of numbers (fewer than 1 percent), the Christians were able to punch above their weight thanks to the trade links and connections in high places. But the promising Azuchi era came to an abrupt end in 1582 when Nobunaga was betrayed by one of his generals, who attacked him in a temple in Kyoto where he was staying with a handful of men. Wounded by an arrow, the overlord fought on desperately before committing seppuku as the temple burned around him. "There did not remain even a small hair which was not reduced to dust and ashes," writes Frois. His assailant sacked the whole of Azuchi for good measure, including castle, town and seminary, but within days the killer was himself killed following a battle with a loyalist named Toyotomi Hideyoshi, who took over the reins of power. The next stage in my journey was to take me into the glittering Momoyama age (1582–98), known for its opulence and dazzling achievements. For the Jesuit mission, though, trouble lay in store.

Chapter Four

Commandments
(Hakata)

Encounters

The train to Fukuoka deposits the passenger, confusingly, at
Hakata. In the orderly world of Japan, this is a rare instance of a
station that bears a different name from its city, and it has to do
with the merging in 1889 of two towns on either side of a river.
The resulting metropolis was named Fukuoka, though Hakata
kept the name of the bay and got the station. Bordered on three
sides by mountains, the modern city has the eighth largest population in the country, nearing one and a half million. The bustling dynamism, friendly people and attractive architecture have
made it "Japan's best-kept secret" for so long now that it must
surely rank as one of the worst-kept in the whole Far East.

Facing the Asian mainland, Hakata Bay was in times past
the arrival point for newcomers from the continent. Sites date
back to the Yayoi era, and some have speculated that this must
have been where the ancestors of the Imperial Family "descended
from Heaven." The bay has seen famous departures too: official
missions to Tang China left from here, as did the legendary Ku-
kai on his way to study Esoteric Buddhism. In a later age Eisai
brought back with him the teachings of Rinzai Zen. But far
more than religion has flowed through the harbor here, for in

Nara times it was the gateway to Japan for the Silk Road. From continental shores came exotic goods on their way via the Inland Sea to the country's Kansai heartland: Islamic pottery, Central Asian glassware, Chinese porcelain. Some of the imports were destined to become icons of Japanese culture: somen noodles, the board game of go, and the *biwa* (Japanese lute), which originated in Persia.

"You see the small island over to the left," my friend says. We're standing on the veranda of his bayside apartment looking over a majestic panorama. To our right stand the cranes of the city's port, behind which are ranged high-rises set against a backdrop of surrounding hills. In front of us an expanse of dazzling blue sea is framed by a long promontory that curves out from the mainland to form a large sheltered bay. To our left lies the island to which my friend is pointing, barely a half-mile away.

"That's where the Mongols landed in one of their invasions. Just imagine it: there were over 700 ships in 1274 and an amazing 4,500 when they came back in 1281. They would have rolled right over the Japanese but for the famous kamikaze (divine wind)." In the bright spring sunshine the island seems surprisingly close. It must have been a hell of a divine wind, I think to myself.

Like the Mongols, the Catholic mission too received a rough reception in Hakata. In 1558 Father Balthazar Gago was granted a license to preach, and the Portuguese priest had just set up a chapel with the aid of Brother Fernandez when rebels seized the city. The missionaries intended to flee by boat to Hirado, but on the way they were robbed by the captain of all their possessions—even their clothes. Somehow they managed to return to Hakata, where there found refuge and kimonos. The rebels planned to take the pair kidnap in return for a ransom of guns and ammunition, so for fifty days they laid low before escaping in women's clothing and large straw hats. Middle-aged Europeans posing as Japanese women is something to ponder, but the ploy proved successful and the pair escaped to Bungo.

It's not for this, however, that I have come to Hakata, but to investigate an encounter that took place in 1587. The people involved were on the one hand Toyotomi Hideyoshi (1536–98), successor to Nobunaga, and on the other Father Gaspar Coelho (1530–90), head of the Jesuit mission in Japan. The occasion was Hideyoshi's victory over his Kyushu enemies, which effectively completed unification of the country. It meant the new leader could turn his attention to the grandiose scheme of invading Korea and China. I gazed northwards over the sea towards continental Asia, perhaps as Hideyoshi himself once did, and wondered what had been going through his mind. Victorious head of armor-clad samurai, he must have felt invincible indeed if he harbored thoughts of conquering China.

The meeting with Coelho was a minor matter for Hideyoshi, but for the Christian cause it was to prove a turning point. Here in Hakata notice was served for the first time that the clash of East and West was going to turn nasty. The man at the center of the drama is arguably the most fascinating figure in Japanese history, not least because he was the first and only person to rise from peasant to be supreme leader. Shrewd, open and affable, Hideyoshi had exceptional military and political skills. He was devious too, and was said to be at his most dangerous when being the most friendly. As a youth he had worked as footman in the service of Nobunaga, who nicknamed him Saru (Monkey) for his looks. The zeal he showed in his job—he warmed his master's straw sandals by pressing them against his body—gained him favor and he was rapidly promoted. Given command of his own troops, he rose to be one of his master's most trusted generals. At the time of Nobunaga's assassination he was on campaign in the west but rushed back to Kyoto to engage the usurper in battle. Following his victory, he assumed leadership of the country.

A contemporary of England's Queen Elizabeth, Hideyoshi had much in common with her larger-than-life father, Henry VIII, despite the obvious disparity in birth. Both were dominating figures given to angry outbursts, both had an eye for pretty women, and both were much concerned about their succession. The two men were notable patrons and practitioners of the arts: Henry danced and composed music, while Hideyoshi performed Noh and studied the tea ceremony. Yet both men also had a ruthless streak and did not hesitate to order the execution of close relatives and advisors. Though they ruled on opposite sides of the world, both were troubled by the power of Roman Catholicism and took action against it for their own ends. One sought to have himself deified; the other made himself head of his national church.

Hideyoshi was at first content to continue the policies of his predecessor towards the Christians. Like Nobunaga, the new leader enjoyed the company of Europeans and wanted the trade contacts. In Kyoto *Namban* fashion was at its height, and some of the nobles wore Portuguese pantaloons and sported crosses. Hideyoshi himself occasionally wore Western clothes and ate beef. He even gave Christian names to his servants because he thought they sounded quaint. He gave permission to the Jesuits to set up a seminary at the foot of his castle in Osaka, and when he paid them a visit he declared that, "Well do I know that the padres are better than the Bonze, for you maintain a different purity of life. . . . I feel no other obstacle to becoming a Christian than its prohibition against keeping many wives." (Henry VIII famously had six wives; Hideyoshi had a principal consort and secondary wives all at the same time.)

After his victory in the Kyushu campaign, Hideyoshi established a base at the Hakozaki Shrine in Hakata, where he stayed for some twenty days. No doubt he gave thanks to its deity Hachiman, the *kami* of war. Here at the shrine the military leader engaged in poetry contests with his generals and received the congratulations of visitors, one of whom was Gaspar Coelho. The shrine faced onto Hakata Bay, and the Jesuit Superior arrived from Nagasaki aboard a *fusta* (a narrow ship with a shallow draft). It was not only well armed but supposedly the fastest vessel in Japan. With him he brought gifts including wine, and the two men shared a picnic. Hideyoshi asked to go aboard Coelho's boat and wanted to inspect a larger Portuguese vessel moored at Hirado, but was told it was impracticable to bring it around because of the shallows. The men parted on good terms, and as on previous occasions Hideyoshi showed his goodwill by gifting land to the Jesuits. He had good reason, for the mission had thrown their weight behind his campaign, and four Christian daimyo had fought with him.

Imagine then the shock when news came that an enraged Hideyoshi was accusing Christians of serious crimes. The principal charge was that they were disrupting social harmony through forced conversions and the destruction of temples. There were other accusations too, namely that in contravention of Buddhist precepts the missionaries had encouraged the eating of horses and cows; that they had duped people by using "special knowledge" of science and medicine; and that they had participated in the trading of Japanese as slaves. (Historians consider that of all the charges the last is the least justified, for the more than 30,000 Japanese sold abroad in these years were in fact traded by daimyo in exchange for gunpowder and other goods. The Jesuits may have known of the trade, but there is no evidence of their involvement.)

Expulsion edict

On July 24, 1587, an edict was issued ordering the expulsion of missionaries. Twenty days to leave the country! It was a bolt from the blue, as unexpected as it was devastating. The Christians had previously enjoyed the leader's patronage; all of a sudden their religion was cast as evil. The edict went to some pains to point out that it was specifically targeted at the *bateren* rather than Europeans in general, and as can be seen in the clauses below it was not intended to harm trade.

1. Japan is a land of *kami* (*kami no kuni*). The propagation from the Kirishitan countries of the pernicious teaching is to be rejected.

2. It is unheard of to approach people in our provinces and make them destroy Shinto shrines and Buddhist temples. The granting of provinces, districts, estates and stipends is dependent on observing the laws of the central government, and these should always be honored. But to corrupt and stir up the lower classes is outrageous.

3. It is the judgment of the central authorities that since the *bateren* are able to direct parishioners as they wish by means of their cunning doctrine, it has led to a violation of Buddhist law in this Land of the Sun (Japan). That being unacceptable, the *bateren* will not be allowed to remain on Japanese soil, and within twenty days they must make preparations to return to their country. If villains from the lower orders make unwarranted trouble for the *bateren* during this time, it will be considered criminal behavior.

4. The purpose of the Black Ships is trade, and that is a different matter. With the passage of time, trade of all kinds may be carried out.

5. From now on all those who do not disturb Buddhism may freely travel to the Kirishitan Country (i.e. Portugal) and return back again. This includes merchants as a matter of course, but also others as well.

On hearing this, the priests were in turmoil: it seemed forty years of mission work was to be in vain. Christianity had been persecuted at a local level before, but this was the first time at a national level and in their bewilderment they sought an explanation. Was it something Coelho had said? Was Hideyoshi angered by the refusal to bring the Portuguese carrack from Hirado? Or was it simply, as rumor had it, annoyance at the refusal of Christian women to sleep with him on religious grounds?

Suspicion eventually centered on a Buddhist physician, Seiyaku-in, who acted as right-hand man to Hideyoshi. Known for his anti-Christian views, he procured women for his master as well as attending to him medically. Following Coelho's departure, the two men are thought to have spent the evening together drinking, during which time Seiyaku-in may have fed Hideyoshi stories of Christian misdeeds. There would have been talk of military connections and how Nagasaki had become a foreign fortification. The Kyushu campaign had highlighted Jesuit capabilities, and Coelho's arrival on the well-armed *fusta* underlined the point. It set off alarm bells about the kind of *ikko-ikki* religious uprising that had caused Nobunaga so much trouble, and Hideyoshi moved swiftly to take preemptive action. A religion of individual salvation was proving to be something more sinister—a threat to his security.

Eager to find local views of the matter, I made inquiries at a Catholic church, but no one there appeared to have given it much thought. I turned instead to the city museum, where the history section had this to say:

> Hakata was struck by fire many times in the many wars that developed among the warring of feudal lords. Toyotomi Hideyoshi, who defeated the Shimazu clan in 1587 and conquered Kyushu, stayed at Chikuzen Hakozaki in June that year on his way

back. Looking over the devastated town of Hakata from a *fusta* ship, Hideyoshi ordered *machi-wari* or town-planning to reconstruct Hakata, and set forth a policy to facilitate economic reconstruction.

It was a reminder of just how marginal Christian matters were in the greater flow of Japanese history: far from being immersed in a "Christian century," Hakata citizens were preoccupied with reconstruction. From the city's viewpoint, the *fusta* had little to do with the anti-Christian edict but with overcoming the legacy of civil disruption.

Since the museum experts had no light to shed on Hideyoshi's motives, I turned instead to a professor at one of the local universities. "You have to understand Hideyoshi was obsessed with power," he told me. "Japan had been unstable for a hundred years, and there were many powerful factions. He needed unity and absolute loyalty for the conquest of China, which was his next project. He was worried that the Christians might not be reliable. You can see that in his treatment of Takayama Ukon. It wasn't his religion he was worried about. It was his allegiance."

In popular memory Takayama Ukon is the shining exemplar of a Christian samurai (he's currently a candidate for canonization). Baptised at the age of twelve when his father converted, he backed Nobunaga in the jostling for power that characterized the age and was rewarded with a domain at Takatsuki (near modern-day Osaka). To make the populace convert, he closed down temples and shrines so that Christian preachers could fill the void. Within eight years, 18,000 out of a population of 25,000 had been baptised. When he was given a larger domain at Akashi, the populace there were fearful of being similarly coerced.

"Ukon was not the only Christian daimyo to force conversion," the professor continued. "But he was known as the leading Christian in Kansai, and he was an important general of Hideyoshi. He funded the seminary at Azuchi Castle, and he was the chief backer of the missionaries in the region. Of all the Christian daimyo, we can be certain he was a true believer. The others, it's not so sure. But Ukon showed strong principles. At Nobunaga's funeral he refused to light an incense stick or say the prayers because they were Buddhist. Hideyoshi wanted to test his loyalty, so he ordered Ukon to give up his faith. When he refused, it proved that his loyalty to Hideyoshi wasn't absolute, so he was stripped of his lands. It was a warning to others, who fell into line. Another general, Konishi Yukinaga, swore to Hideyoshi to give up his faith, but in fact carried on believing and shielding missionaries. Ukon was the only one to refuse."

There was another factor in Hideyoshi's edict, the professor explained: money. His military adventures were financially demanding, and the invasion of Korea was going to cost a whole lot more. Again the comparison with Henry VIII comes to mind, for the English king took advantage of the split with Rome to seize the assets of Catholic monasteries. In Hideyoshi's case, he moved to confiscate Nagasaki from the Jesuits, and with it the accruing fees from the lucrative Portuguese trade. No wonder he took pains to insist the merchants would not be affected by his edict!

Military ties

The mesh of military and religious ties that upset Hideyoshi had been evident at a previous meeting with the Jesuits, which took place at Osaka Castle in 1586. Anyone familiar with the reconstruction that stands at the heart of the modern city will know just how impressive the moated headquarters must have been. Five hundred thousand rocks were used in the ramparts, many of which brought from the Inland Sea. There were gilded tiles on the seven-story main tower, and its walls were decorated with large reliefs of a crouching tiger. The Jesuit Superior led a thirty-man delegation, and the Japanese leader had been charm personified. "He acted as guide just as if he were a private individual," wrote Frois, who was there that day.

> And so in this way he led us up to the seventh story, describing on the way all the riches that were stored away in each floor. . . . Then he began to go down by other stairs and he showed us the place where he normally slept. . . . He sat down and ordered the saké to be brought in. This he took with his own hands and served to Father Coelho. . . . Then they brought him the fish, which is taken as an accompaniment to the saké; he took up the chopsticks and with his own hands served it out to the Fathers and Brothers. Such was the extreme kindness and favor which he showed to Father Coelho and his companions that all who saw or heard about it declared that he had never done anything like it before.

During the discussions Hideyoshi raised the topic of Korea and wondered about the possibility of using two large Portuguese ships for the invasion. Coelho not only said he would help secure them, but even mentioned the possibility of Spanish-led forces from the Philippines aiding in the attack. Hideyoshi suggested in return he would set up churches all across China. A happy alliance was in the making, and Hideyoshi issued a charter allowing the Jesuits to preach anywhere in Japan—a significant move given the hostility among many daimyo.

Yet despite the shared interests, things went badly awry at Hakata, and Coelho's subsequent behavior served to confirm the very worst fears of the Japanese. In response to the expulsion order he planned to hold Nagasaki by force, while soliciting the support of Christian daimyo. When they demurred, he sent abroad to see if military assistance was forthcoming from the Spanish or Portuguese. Though it all came to nothing, it illustrated the potential to turn to armed force. One is used to scheming Jesuits in portrayals of Elizabethan England: here on the other side of the world similar plots were being hatched.

In the event, the mission escaped relatively lightly from the Hakata edict. Nagasaki was taken out of Jesuit hands, and some sixty of their 250 institutions were destroyed, including the grand Namban-ji (Southern Barbarian Temple) of Kyoto. On the other hand, of the 120 missionaries who gathered in Kyushu for expulsion, only three junior members actually departed— and they returned to Japan after training abroad. Others went into hiding or took to the safety of domains held by Christian daimyo. As time passed Hideyoshi's anger seemed to cool, and he turned his attention to other matters—preparations for invading Korea, for instance.

As it turned out, the post-Hakata years proved surprisingly good for the Catholic cause. In 1589, just two years after the expulsion order, the Jesuits made 10,000 new converts, the most famous of whom was Hosokawa Gracia (1563–1600). A noblewoman, elegant yet resolute, she's portrayed in the iconography as a counterpart to Takayama Ukon, a long-suffering female to stand alongside the stalwart samurai. *A Samurai's Wife: Love, Strife and Faith* runs the title of a popular novel about her. Her unhappy fate was to be the daughter of Akechi Mitsuhide, Nobunaga's assassin, following whose death she suffered disgrace. Anxious to distance himself, her husband held her in confinement, during which time she was influenced by a maid from a Christian family and secretly visited Father Organtino in the church at Osaka. Even after the Hakata edict, she remained determined to join the faith and had herself baptised at home by her maid.

Reports of such activities must have reached Hideyoshi, but he showed surprisingly little animosity towards Christians in these years (he never actually banned the religion). He even seemed indifferent to the fact that missionaries had disobeyed his edict and were continuing their work. "I will not permit any man of honor to become a Christian," he said, "but I do not object if they are old or of the lower rank, because such people cannot harm my country." In a letter to the viceroy of India, he explained that Christianity had upset the religious order of his country and destroyed feudal ties of subject and vassal. He also wrote to the Spanish governor of the Philippines that they had no more right to spread their religion in Japan than the Japanese had to spread theirs in Manila—a fair point, one might say. Particularism was kicking back against universalism.

Adaptation

Three years after the Hakata incident, Hideyoshi received a large delegation at Osaka Castle to honor four young Japanese Christians returning from Rome. The seventeen priests in attendance were led by the head of the Jesuits in Asia, Alessandro Valignano (1539–1606). Diplomatically, he came not as a cleric but as the official envoy of the Portuguese viceroy of India. The delegation was intended to make an impression, with lavish gifts and elaborate outfits: even the Negro servants were decked out in velvet liveries and gold chains. The meeting went well, for Hideyoshi was eager to hear the stories of the four youths and was much entertained by their playing music on harpsichord and other European instruments. One of the young priests in attendance, Joao Rodrigues, later wrote an account of the episode:

> It was in the castle and palace of Juraku that Taiko [Hideyoshi] received an embassy which the viceroy of India, Dom Duarte de Menezes, had sent with rich presents. The ambassador was Father Visitor Ales-

sandro Valignano, and he was accompanied by many Portuguese and the four Japanese nobles, dressed in our fashion, who had been to Rome. The reception was one of the most solemn events of Japan at that time, for the principal nobility and grandees of the kingdom were present. He ordered that the whole city should line the route of the ambassador, who traveled in a litter while the Portuguese and the Japanese nobles rode on fine richly caparisoned horses.

The four young Japanese had been dispatched by Valignano eight years previously with two objectives: to raise awareness of Japan in Europe in order to secure funds and personnel for the mission; and to raise awareness among Japanese of the glories of the European Church. The youths were treated in Europe as celebrities from an exotic empire on the far side of the world that would soon be Christian. They not only met with the king of Spain and other top dignitaries but in Rome were able to present the pope with a standing screen painted by the top Japanese artist of the age, Kano Eitoku, which had been given to them by Nobunaga. In all they visited seventy cities and created a sensation wherever they went. It had been a journey into the unknown, with unexpected culture stress: they had felt uncomfortable on high chairs with legs dangling in the air and were almost traumatized at having to dance with female partners. There's a portrait of them in Augsburg in 1586, which shows them done up in European finery, with brocaded jackets and neck frills. East had gone West, and here in these Japanese Christians was the result.

The man responsible for the project, Alessandro Valignano, had achieved the position of Visitor, answerable only to the Jesuit head in Rome, at the remarkably young age of thirty-four. He was unusual in being an Italian in a Portuguese-dominated order, and he was unusual too in appearance, for he was tall enough to turn heads in Europe while in Japan he drew an excited crowd wherever he went. He was a giant culturally as well as physically, for at a time when ethnocentrism was the norm he implemented a policy of adaptation, by which Jesuits were expected to conform to Japanese ways. It might be self-evident nowadays, but at the time it was a revolutionary move. Like other Europeans, missionaries looked down on the local culture: sitting on the floor and eating raw fish was seen as degrading, as if they had sunk to the level of heathens. However, this is exactly what Valignano insisted on, as a result of which priests who had come to change Japan had to change themselves. To the disgust of some, the Jesuits were turning Japanese!

Valignano was based in Macao, but he focused his attention on Japan and made three separate and lengthy visits. Like Xavier before him, he had high expectations of the country. In *Summary of Things Japanese* (1583), Valignano stressed that though the people did everything in the opposite manner to Europeans, it by no means meant they were uncivilized. The country boasted exquisite temples, as well as sophisticated levels of craftsmanship. Artists such as Sesshu had produced paintings of a stunning quality, while the fighting skills of the samurai were considered the best in Asia. Along with this went an educated and orderly populace—"they excel not only all the other Oriental peoples, they surpass the Europeans as well," he wrote. It must have shocked some of his readers. "Even the common folk and peasants are well brought up and are so remarkably polite that they give the impression that they were trained at court," he went on. Their sole fault, it seemed, was a lack of Christianity.

Pragmatism

For the Jesuits to be effective, Valignano saw the necessity for good language skills, and he set up seminary courses to that end.

Learning Japanese had previously been considered too difficult and a waste of valuable time. Valignano saw things differently: "They have but one language, and it is the best, the most elegant the most copious in the known world," he pronounced. Although lack of Japanese had hampered the mission in early days, progress was swift after the introduction of the new system. In 1586 only fourteen out of twenty-seven padres were able to listen to confessions; by 1592 not only could thirty-seven of the forty-two padres listen to confession, but ten of them were also able to preach. The language learning process was greatly facilitated after 1590 when Valignano arrived with the four young envoys from Goa, for he brought with him a printing press, which was set to work turning out dictionaries, grammar books and readers. The once formidable language barrier had been cut down to size.

Up to this point no Japanese converts had ever been given high positions in the mission, because they were seen as untrustworthy and incapable of grasping theology. Valignano, however, thought that if Christianity was to become a Japanese religion, it would require native priests. Accordingly he set up training courses, and the number of Japanese Jesuits increased from twenty in 1583 to seventy in 1593. (It was not until 1601 that the first native priests were ordained.) At the same time, there was an expansion of lay assistants *(dojuku)* and caretaker-helpers *(kambo)*, drawn from Japanese ranks. The reforms extended to Church matters too, one example being the Eucharist, for which congregations were not expected to stand because respect in Japan was normally shown by lowering oneself. In this way Valignano sought to make Christianity less of a foreign affair and more of a Japanese religion.

Another of Valignano's innovations was to model the Jesuits on the hierarchical structure of Zen monasteries. The rationale was to enable the mission to reach out to all levels of Japanese society, which esteemed those at the top and looked down on those at the bottom. In taking their message to the poor, the Jesuits had been alienating those who were offended by the association with social inferiors. If the Jesuits had differentiated ranks, it would enable them to relate to all sections of society, since people would feel comfortable dealing with someone commensurate with their standing. In compromises of this kind, the Visitor was skating on thin ground, as the Rites Controversy in China was to show in the 1630s. To orthodox Catholics, such policies were akin to supping with the devil.

Accusations of devil worship were in fact never far from Catholic lips. Father Vilela, for instance, found Shinto animism hard to account for and wrote that, "The devil has brought people to such a state that they also worship many ridiculous things: some there are who worship foxes, while others worship snakes, cows, deer, tortoises, posts and stones." Frois wrote of how he and Coelho had once smashed for firewood some "intricate, exquisitely made" Buddhist statues because they were idolatrous, and under Jesuit influence the daimyo of Arima had destroyed over forty Buddhist and Shinto institutions in the belief they were evil. Unsurprisingly, such attitudes provoked hostility, and here again Valignano proved revolutionary: "We must show great love for the Buddhist bonzes," he wrote. "We should especially refrain from rejoicing at their misfortunes, despising them and saying bad things against them. This attitude is particularly disliked by Japanese; not only does it not raise our prestige, but it gives us a bad reputation."

Valignano's intention in all this was pragmatic, for he wanted to advance the Jesuit cause (he made every effort to keep other Catholic orders out of Japan). Things went smoother if you did them the Japanese way, he realized. In similar vein he took exception to the military intrigues of Gaspar Coelho because they could so easily backfire, so to speak, and his intervention forced the Superior into resigning. Thereafter the Jesuits pledged to keep out of political involvements. In this way, thanks to Valignano, they were able to steer a way through the stormy waters of the 1590s.

When Hideyoshi launched the Korean invasion in 1592, the leading general was the Christian Konishi Yukinaga (1555–1600) who developed a rivalry with Kato Kiyomasa, a Nichiren zealot. The two armies made their way up the peninsula in a pincer movement, meeting up in Seoul, where friction became apparent: Kato's troops carried banners with "Nam Myoho Renge Kyo" (Glory to the Lotus Sutra), while Konishi's troops had crosses and were accompanied by a European missionary. The invaders pushed on northwards towards the border, but were stalled by Chinese resistance while at the same time suffering naval losses that cut their supplies. As a result Konishi was forced to negotiate a humiliating truce, and back in Japan he and Kato became fractious neighbors. While the former promoted Christianity in his domain, the latter persecuted them in his. It was an omen of things to come.

Tea matters

Hakozaki Shrine, where Hideyoshi stayed in 1587, faces towards Korea and bears a message of menacing intent, TEKIKOKU FUKOU—MAY ENEMY COUNTRIES SUBMIT. Though directed at Mongolian invaders, no doubt Hideyoshi identified with the sentiment. While at the shrine he engaged in poetry contests with his generals and took tea with his master of ceremonies, Sen no Rikyu. I had read of a "kettle-hanging pine tree" where the event took place and went in search. It turned out, surprisingly, to be fifteen minutes walk away in the grounds of Kyushu University Hospital. The tree would once have stood in unspoiled surrounds, bordering the sea, and it was a reminder of how greatly shrine precincts have shrunk in modern times. Rikyu had no doubt combed the area for a suitable location after being given the order to prepare tea, and he chose a tree by the beach, where he lit a fire of carefully arranged pine needles beneath a low branch, from which he hung the kettle. It was all in keeping with the aesthetics of *wabi cha*, a style of tea that thrives on minimalism and rustic simplicity.

It's been said that in perfecting the tea ceremony Rikyu was influenced by the Catholic Mass, an assertion that seems at first ridiculous given the ceremony's quintessential Japaneseness. Yet Christians were active in the circles in which Rikyu mixed, and at least two of his Seven Disciples were converts (his wife and daughter too, it's rumored). A modern-day descendant of the tea master, Sen Soshitsu, has argued persuasively for the Catholic influence, and once the connection is pointed out the similarities are striking. Raising the tea to head height as a token of respect, for instance, and wiping the bowl after drinking with a white cloth. There is indeed in the whole ritual a sense of two or three gathering together in spiritual union. Could the *okashi* (Japanese confectionary) that accompanies the green tea have been inspired by the wafer that accompanies wine in the Mass? Food for thought, indeed . . .

Tea was one of the few native pastimes that the missionaries did not find sinful, and they even used the tea rooms of prominent Japanese for religious ceremonies. Valignano stipulated that every Jesuit residence should have a tea room for entertaining visitors, and missionaries cultivated the practice as a means of engaging with the elite—the sixteenth-century equivalent of golf. The Portuguese priest Joao Rodrigues (1558–1633), known as "the Interpreter," developed a keen understanding of the practice, and in his book on Japanese culture he wrote four chapters that constitute the first full account by a foreigner. The purpose, he wrote, was for Japanese "to contemplate within their souls with all peace and modesty the things they see there and thus through their own efforts to understand the mysteries." In the quiet of the tea room, over a bowl of hot whipped green tea, Jesuit and Japanese could come together in the pursuit of perfection. Within the stillness of the tearoom lay common ground, as if East and West were drinking from the same spiritual source.

Meanwhile, in the world outside, trouble was brewing.

Top left: Wakasa of Tanegashima, whose "shotgun wedding" with a Portuguese merchant may have helped secure Western firearms. **Top right:** Francis Xavier statue at Ichiuji Castle, Kagoshima, where the missionary went to speak with the feudal lord. **Bottom:** 26 Martyrs Memorial on Nishizaka Hill, Nagasaki. The smaller figures denote the three youths crucified. The youngest was just twelve.

Juan of Goto, one of the 26 Martyrs of 1597.

Top: Entrance to the ruined Azuchi Castle, Nobunaga Oda's stronghold. **Bottom:** "Unzen hell": Christians were tortured in its volcanic waters in the 1630s.

Top left: Amakusa Shiro statue at Hara Castle, where the uprising he led was brutally put down. **Top right:** Amakusa Shiro contemporary style, as depicted at a bus stop in Amakusa. **Bottom:** Bastian's hut at Sotome. Bastian, short for "Sebastian," developed a calendar to track the dates of Christian festivals by converting from the solar-based system of Europe to the lunar-based method used in Japan.

Top left: Copies of Bastian's calendar (Ikitsuki Museum). **Top right:** "Southern Barbarian"—the name given to Europeans when they first arrived in Japan—at the port of Kuchinotsu in Shimabara. **Bottom left:** Chalice made in Japan. At first, Catholics imported religious goods from Europe, but Japanese artisans soon learned to produce high-quality items. (courtesy of Francisco no Ie, Kyoto). **Bottom right:** Sword guard with Madonna and Child (courtesy of Francisco no Ie, Kyoto).

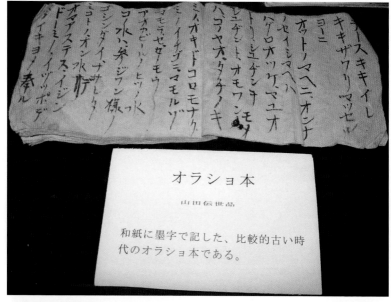

Top: Manuscript of *orashio*, or Hidden Christian prayers (Ikitsuki Museum). **Bottom left:** Maria Kannon, in which the bodhisattva Kannon is used to represent the Virgin Mary (courtesy of Francisco no Ie, Kyoto). **Bottom right:** Kirishitan lantern showing an image of the Madonna at its base, which was covered up in the time of persecution (courtesy of Francisco no Ie, Kyoto).

Top: Replica of the Amakusa printing press, brought to Japan by the Jesuits in 1590 (Amakusa Collegio Museum). **Bottom:** Hidden Christians at prayer (exhibit in the Rosario Kan at Oe).

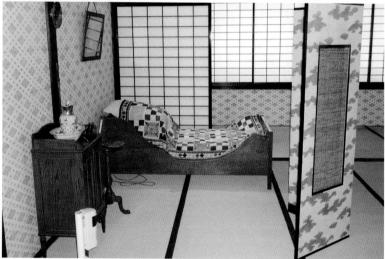

Top: Model of Dejima in the Edo period, with a small bridge connecting to the mainland. Dutch traders were restricted to the artificial island after the Tokugawa shogunate closed the country to Europeans. **Bottom:** Dutch bed placed on tatami mats in Dejima.

Top: Sotome coastline where *Silence* is set. In the foreground is a memorial commemorating the novel, and in the background can be seen the Endo Shusaku Literary Museum.
Bottom left: *Fumie* showing Maria, or Mary. Such images were stepped on in a ritual of renunciation to flush out Hidden Christians (courtesy of Francisco no Ie, Kyoto).
Bottom right: Endo Shusaku, author of *Silence* (Endo Shusaku Literary Museum).

Top: Dozaki Church in Lower Goto, where a Hidden Christian community survived the repression of Tokugawa times. **Bottom:** Monument in Goto showing Hidden Christians in discussion after learning of the presence of a French priest in Nagasaki.

Hidden Christian cave in Upper Goto, with statue of Jesus.

The present Oura Church at Nagasaki. **Insert:** Father Petitjean statue at Oura Church, Nagasaki. The French priest was the first to encounter the Hidden Christians after the ending of Japan's isolationism.

Top left: Hidden Christian baptism vase. The stick was used to sprinkle water on the head of those being baptised. **Top right:** Hidden Christian altar, or *nando* (Ikitsuki Museum). **Bottom:** Hidden Christian baptism in modern times (used by permission of Ikitsuki Museum).

Top: Danjiku Christian hideout on Ikitsuki Island. **Bottom:** Ikitsuki Hidden Christians collecting baptism water (Ikitsuki Museum). **Left:** Memorial to Gaspar Nishi, the samurai who became leader of the Christian community on Ikitsuki Island in 1599. He was later arrested and put to death.

Top left: Collection of heads from Urakami Cathedral, which was destroyed by the atom bomb dropped on Nagasaki. **Top right:** Kawakami Shigetsugu, modern-day champion of Hidden Christians, on Neshiko beach. **Bottom:** Interfaith ceremony at Karematsu Jinja, Sotome, attended by Catholics, Hidden Christians, and Buddhists.

Chapter Five

Crucifixion
(Nagasaki)

Martyrs Museum

Ten years after the Hakata jolt came a bloody aftershock with the crucifixion of twenty-six Christians in Nagasaki, intended as a public warning that the religion had overstepped the mark. No longer could the seriousness of the situation be doubted, for lives were—quite literally—at stake. Individual belief was enmeshed with international politics, for as well as twenty Japanese the executed included four Spaniards, one Mexican and one Portuguese Goan. The coming of Christianity had developed into more than a simple clash of values—it had become a matter of life and death. The result was a gruesome drama that started in Kansai and ended in Nagasaki.

If you arrive in the city by train, you see a hill to the left as you exit the station, which lies across a busy thoroughfare and takes just a few minutes to reach. It's Nishizaka Hill, and the small park there marks the site of the crucifixions. Once it was open land overlooking the city, but in modern times it has been swallowed up in the closely packed hillside housing. The patch of greenery that remains contains an idiosyncratic church with brightly colored towers and a long horizontal monument showing twenty-six crucified figures. Look closely and you notice three of them are markedly smaller than the rest: they represent the three teenagers among the crucified—the youngest was just twelve.

Appropriately enough, it was Easter Sunday when I visited, and I sat for a while on a bench to soak in the atmosphere. It's thought that over six hundred people in all were executed on this hill, but the scene around me was humdrum. Two young girls on a trip chatting about souvenirs. An elderly couple inspecting the cherry blossoms. A sumo-sized man walking a toy poodle. Farther up the hill stood an enormous statue of Kannon, smiling beatifically over the bay below. Taken all in all, it was a typically Japanese scene and hard to square with the events of the past. "Today I want to be one of the many pilgrims who come to the Martyrs' Hill here in Nagasaki, to the place where Christians sealed their fidelity to Christ with the sacrifice of their lives," said John Paul II on a visit in 1981. Yet here on this Easter Sunday there were few signs of pilgrims.

At the back of the park stands the 26 Martyrs Museum. It was put together by Diego Yuuki (1922–2008), a Spanish Jesuit who arrived in Japan in 1948 and ran the museum for forty-six years. There's an endearingly eclectic air about it: a book from Mexico dating from the time of the martyrdoms; a bronze statue of Jesus donated by the Knights of Columbus; an ancient camphor root exhibited because it looks "tortured." There are too some interesting Hidden Christian items from the time of persecution, but the museum's most prized exhibit is a letter by Francis Xavier to the Portuguese king. The top half is in perfect calligraphy, though farther down the saint betrays his human side with a notable slant.

The heart of the exhibition belongs to the 26 Martyrs, whose story is told in a booklet painstakingly researched by Diego Yuuki. It begins with the arrival in 1593 of the Franciscans, a mendicant order that cherished poverty after the model of

Francis of Assisi. Founded in the fourteenth century, the order kept its reputation for integrity even though corruption in the Catholic Church was rife. Its friars had traveled westward on the coattails of the Spanish as they pushed across the Atlantic, crossing Mexico and pushing on to the Philippines. From there they cast an envious eye on opportunities in Japan. The division of the world into Spanish and Portuguese spheres had been restated by a papal decree of 1585, which confirmed the Jesuit monopoly in Japan. Reports reaching Manila suggested they were making a mess of things through their involvement in trade and military matters, regarded as anathema by the pure-minded Franciscans.

In 1593, the Spanish governor of the Philippines sent a delegation headed by a Franciscan friar named Pedro Bautisto to negotiate relations with Japan. He was accompanied by three others of his order, and during the negotiations the group petitioned Hideyoshi for permission to build a monastery. Desirous of trade ties with Manila, the Japanese leader showed his goodwill by donating an estate to them in Kyoto on which they built a monastery. There's a drawing of it in the small museum that now stands on the site, and it shows walled grounds, a school, living quarters and two small hospitals (one for lepers). The locals called it Namban-ji (Southern Barbarian Temple) after the first city church, though the official name was Los Angeles. The Spanish touch was an exotic addition to a city alive with rebuilding and revitalization.

Unlike the Jesuits, who were keeping a low profile following the Hakata edict, the Franciscans were open about proselytizing and their charitable works soon attracted followers. The concentration of Christians that developed around their building came in time to be known as "Dios-machi," or "God's Town." The breach of monopoly upset the Jesuits, who also took exception to the lack of discretion, and they agitated behind the scenes against the newcomers. For their part, the Franciscans were shocked by the compromises Jesuits had made with Japanese ways, such as using silk sheets and providing lavish banquets for honored guests. The sectional rivalry was compounded by a national divide, for the Jesuits were mostly Portuguese and distrusted the close ties of the Franciscans with the Spanish.

The mutual accusations alarmed the Japanese, and matters came to a head in 1596 when a Spanish galleon named the *San Felipe* was blown off course on its way from Manila to Mexico and shipwrecked off Shikoku. Its valuable cargo of silk and brocades spilled into the Bay of Urago, where they spread over the water like a sodden carpet. There was a sizable portion of gold on board too, and the cargo was seized by local authorities while the crew was detained. Angered by the treatment, the pilot told his captors that they had better be careful, since the Spanish would colonize their country just as they had South America. "The missionaries come as the king of Spain's advance guard," he warned them. Since his ship had contained both military and missionaries, the threat was all too credible.

When word reached Hideyoshi, he reacted furiously by not only renewing the Hakata expulsion edict but ordering a roundup of Kansai's leading Christians. A list of some 4,000 was made, from which Jesuits were eliminated for fear of disrupting Portuguese trade. Instead, Franciscans were targeted. Numbers were further reduced by the intercession of sympathizers, and in the end just twenty-four people were seized in Osaka and Kyoto. Among them was Pedro Bautisto, who remained confident of the Japanese leader's goodwill. "We have nothing to fear while Hideyoshi is alive," he claimed. How wrong he was!

By this time, the Japanese leader was aging and increasingly erratic. He had acted with unpredictable ruthlessness on previous occasions: in 1591 he forced his tea master Sen no Rikyu to commit suicide, and in 1595 he turned against his nephew-successor Hidetsugu, whose whole household was put to death. Now the Japanese leader decided the arrested Christians should all be put to death, and the rationale was written on a board to be paraded before them to the site of execution:

> These men came from the Philippines with the title of ambassadors, but they remained in Kyoto preaching the Christian religion that I rigorously prohibited in past years. I thus command that they be executed along with the Japanese who have joined their religion. So these twenty-four will be crucified in Nagasaki. Let all know that I again issue a prohibition against the religion. If anyone dares to disobey this order, they will be punished together with their family.

Was it concern about Japan's security that motivated him, or the opportunity to seize some rich plunder? "Don't forget that Hideyoshi needed money for his Korean campaign," the Hakata professor had told me. Valignano, on the other hand, felt that Japanese anxieties about foreign intervention had started in Nobunaga's time, escalated after the Spanish took over the Philippines, and rose even higher with the union of the Spanish and Portuguese crowns in 1580. The *San Felipe* incident simply served to confirm their worst fears. At the same time, the concern about a potential fifth column was noted by a contemporary called Father Passio: "As Hideyoshi believes that there is no other life . . . he has it firmly in his head that it is not salvation that is being sought, but the desire to make many Christians who would unite like brothers and could then easily rise against him." The politicized nature of the Jesuit mission was proving a double-edged sword.

26 Martyrs

In the Martyrs Museum at Nagasaki, there's a large-scale fresco, containing 357 people in all, which tells the story of the crucifixions in a series of tableaux. It begins with the arrests, following which the prisoners' right ears were cut off and the men paraded around Kyoto in carts. (Mutilation was a common form of public humiliation.) The men were exhibited too in Osaka and Sakai, in both of which Christian groups were active. They were then forced to walk the 450 miles to Nagasaki with arms tied behind their backs (Diego Yuuki suggests they rode part of the way), and at each domain border the hundreds of soldiers guarding them had to be changed over. One of the places they passed through was Hakata, where, ironically given Hideyoshi's edict, there was a small but flourishing Christian community.

On the way to Kyushu two volunteers accompanying the group to offer comfort were arrested after being warned to desist. One was just twelve years old. It brought the number of prisoners to twenty-six in all, among whom were men of very diverse backgrounds. The Japanese contingent included a sword smith, silk weaver, saké maker and a former Buddhist priest. Three members of the Jesuit order had been inadvertently arrested too in the chaotic roundup. There was even an unknown man called Mathias, who'd offered himself in place of another Mathias on the wanted list. Of the six foreign Franciscans, five had come to Japan to preach, but the Mexican friar—poor fellow—had been on his way home when the *San Felipe* was shipwrecked, following which he made his way to Kyoto only to be arrested shortly afterwards.

The choice of Nagasaki as the place of execution was a deliberate ploy to strike at the heart of the country's Christians. With its eleven churches, it remained a Jesuit stronghold. But what of crucifixion: was it some kind of black joke that those who followed the cross should die on the cross? In fact it had long been used as a means of execution in Japan, together with burning, beheading and being boiled alive in a pot. "With us there is no crucifixion," Luis Frois had noted in *Topsy-Turvy*. "In Japan, it is something very common." The Japanese style differed from that of the Romans, and a large wooden cross exhibited in the Martyrs Museum demonstrates the difference. In addition to the two horizontal pieces, one for the arms and one for the feet, there is a protruding stump to prop up the torso. Hands and ankles were secured by a clamp, with a rope tied around the waist. An eyewitness account of the gruesome manner of execution has been left by Francesco Carletti:

> The cross is laid on the ground and the body of the sufferer is stretched upon and fixed to it. Then the cross is quickly raised, and its foot being placed in a hole made for the purpose, they prop it up to make it stand firm. This done, the judge who pronounced sentence, who is obliged to be present at its execution, gives the executioner his orders, in accordance with which he [the executioner] pierces the sufferer's body with a spear, thrusting it into the right side upwards through the heart and out above the left shoulder, thus passing through the whole body from one side to the other. And not infrequently two executioners approach, each with his own lance, one piercing one side, and one the other, so that the spears cross one another and both points appear above the shoulders, and death speedily ensues. And if, as occasionally happens, the sufferers do not die as the result of these two first spear wounds, they proceed to stab them in the throat, or on the left side at the point where the heart is, and thus put an end to them.

In the account of the 26 Martyrs given by Diego Yuuki, one of the most striking features is the enthusiasm with which the men go to their deaths. "I firmly believe that to die for Christ is God's greatest gift. What a wonderful way to begin the year!" wrote Pedro Bautisto in prison. When the prisoners reached the site of the execution, they embraced their crosses with joy as if welcoming their fate. The executioner was puzzled by the fervor, and reading Diego Yuuki's account, frankly so was I. For anyone who treasures the gift of life, who sees it as a miracle in itself, the death desire is hard to fathom without an unswerving certainty in the afterlife. Even then it begs the question: why would God create human life if his greatest wish is for people to sacrifice it? Why indeed create the earth at all?

Accounts of the last moments of the martyrs were given by those present, among whom were Luis Frois and Joao Rodriguez. The twelve-year-old was offered his life if he was willing to re-nounce his faith, but he turned down the chance, refusing "to exchange a life that has no end for one that soon finishes." The Mexican friar managed a play on words by pronouncing that Felipe (his name) had been saved by grace of the *San Felipe*. The most famous of the martyrs, the Japanese Jesuit Paul Miki, was known for his eloquence and throughout the long walk from Kyoto he tried to convert those with whom he came into con-tact. Until his arrest, he was on track to become the first native priest, and in a speech from the cross he declared that as a true Japanese with no connection to the Philippines he was innocent of the charges, yet nonetheless was willing to forgive Hideyoshi.

The impact of the crucifixions was not as the authorities had intended. Rather than intimidating the populace, the bravery of the martyrs' deaths served to enhance the appeal of Christianity, as word spread that here was a faith worth dying for. It's thought some 4,000 people attended the event, overwhelming the guards in their eagerness to secure relics, and a seventeenth-century

Mexican painting shows Christian sympathizers holding pieces of cloth beneath the crosses to catch the victims' blood. In the weeks that followed, the bodies were left pinned up as a grim warning to the township below and guards were posted to stop people gathering on the hilltop. In a poignant irony, more than a month after the executions the crew of the *San Felipe* were able to leave Japan and sailed from Nagasaki in full view of the grisly legacy of their unfortunate accident.

End of an era

For the Jesuit mission, the martyrdoms marked the end of an era of optimism, and as if to signify its passing Luis Frois died in Nagasaki a few months afterwards. He had joined the Jesuits at sixteen, knew Xavier and Yajiro when they were in Goa, and arrived at the age of thirty-one in Japan. Six years later he met with Nobunaga in Kyoto, and he remained a firm advocate of the Jesuit top-down strategy: "I always bear in mind the Portuguese proverb, Sweep the stairs from the top," he wrote. "The Japanese cringe and fawn to those above them. . . . That is why evangelizing from the bottom up is ineffectual." As secretary to the Superior, he wrote hundreds of long letters and reports on Japan, in addition to which he produced *Historia de Japam* about the early mission.

Frois was not just a clerical scribe, however, for the reports he wrote were printed and circulated among the European elite as propaganda for the Japan mission. He could thus be claimed as a writer of literary significance, for his accounts constituted a form of travel literature. This was the Age of Discovery, when interest in overseas voyages was high, as demonstrated by the best-selling Richard Haklyut, author of *The Principal Navigations, Voyages, Traffiques and Discoveries of the English Nation* (1589–1600). For Europeans, Japan held a special fascination with its "topsy-turvy culture," and Frois was able to cater to the curiosity thanks to his eye for detail and his capacious memory. His report of the 26 Martyrs turned out to be the last of a remarkable life.

Following the crucifixions, the Catholic Church was in turmoil, as its leaders pondered the situation. Hideyoshi's attitude was unclear: on the one hand he appeared friendly, but on the other he expressed hostility. He wrote in a letter to the governor of Manila that "I have received information that in your kingdoms the preaching of religion is a trick and a deceit with which you subject foreign kingdoms." He was willing to offer friendship, he said, provided no more priests were sent to preach "this strange and false religion." But the Christian problem was not uppermost in his mind, for he was in bad health and preoccupied with bigger matters. His bid to conquer China had stalled, and a great earthquake had shattered the huge Buddha he had built in Kyoto (taller even than the statue of Todaiji). Above all, there was the matter of succession, for his son Hideyori was not yet five years old.

Meanwhile, Hideyoshi's advisor Seiyaku-in continued to intrigue against the Christians. An order was given in 1598 to the governor of Nagasaki to expel all Jesuits, except for two or three needed to minister to Portuguese residents. Once again churches were destroyed, seminaries suppressed and priests forced into hiding. On one occasion, the authorities were deceived by having lay people dressed as priests stand on the deck of a departing vessel, as if the missionaries were leaving the country. Meanwhile, roughly 100 of the 125 Jesuits had gone underground, sheltered by sympathizers and influential Christians. Groups of believers were set up to meet once a week in private houses, and it seemed an era of hidden Christians had begun. Hideyoshi's death shortly afterwards changed the whole situation.

Two weeks before his end, Hideyoshi met with Joao Rodrigues, "the Interpreter." The two men had been friends since

1591, when the young Portuguese had accompanied Valignano at his meeting with Hideyoshi. The friendship had helped shield the Jesuits from greater disaster, and the priest was on such good terms with the Japanese leader that he even tried to persuade him into a deathbed conversion. In the uncharted waters that followed Hideyoshi's death, the role of the Interpreter was to prove crucial in smoothing the Church's path into the new era.

My visit to the Martyrs Museum had taken me into some dark places, and I sought relief by following the small stream of people heading to celebrate Easter in a church adjacent to the park. There was a packed congregation of some two hundred, and I joined those standing at the back. Women wore white veils over their heads in the manner of southern Europeans, and the sole foreigner besides myself was the priest. Had it been like this in the Nagasaki of 1597? The sermon was of joy, resurrection and the 26 Martyrs, the names of whom, the priest declared, will be forever cherished. It struck me this was the Church's equivalent of ancestor worship, and that the communal honoring of saints was similar to that of ancestral *kami* in Shinto. Hideyoshi himself had been apotheosized at Hokoku Shrine in Kyoto, where rites continue to this day to be dedicated to him. In this way both victims and persecutor in the events of 1597 are honored by the larger "family" to which they belonged—on the one hand, a Church with its fathers, brothers and Mother Mary; on the other, a nation with its emperor and shared heroes. In the clash of primal and axial religions, Japaneseness and Christianity vie for ownership of the past.

Chapter Six

Persecution
(Omura)

First Kirishitan daimyo

Omura City, with a population of 80,000, is a modest sort of place. It's notable mainly as the access point for Nagasaki Airport, which is situated on a small island in the middle of the adjacent bay. The huge mass of water looks to be surrounded by land on four sides, and you'd be forgiven for assuming it's a large lake, so calm is its appearance. Barely visible in the northwest corner, however, is a narrow passageway to the sea, which on maps at least gives the bay the shape of a uterus. In the past the watery expanse lay at the center of a domain that stretched down to Nagasaki in the south and embraced offshore islands to the west. It was here that Japan's first Christian daimyo emerged, Omura Sumitada (1522–97). It was his legacy that I'd come to explore, as Japan entered an age of persecution and Christians took to hiding en masse.

The Kirishitan heritage is something of a selling point for the town, and there are tours of related sites. Mine was under the courteous guidance of Mr. Moriguchi, one of the legion of former salarymen eking out a small pension. In his desire for betterment he had developed an enthusiasm for local history, and by way of introduction he took me to the Kirishitan section of the town museum. It turned out to be a disappointingly small room at the library, given over to a handful of tawdry exhibits. One of the walls was devoted to a display about the Four Envoys sent to Rome, for two of the youths had been born locally. The Augsburg portraits were prominently displayed, along with Europeanized names such as Don Julian, which signified their noble birth. Carefully groomed by the Jesuits, three of them had followed the intended path and become priests: one was martyred, one died of illness, one worked in exile in Macao. The fourth, named Miguel, mysteriously gave up Christianity altogether. Considering the Jesuit maxim, "Give me the child until he is seven, and I will give you the man," I was intrigued and asked what had happened to him. "The Omura Historical Committee is investigating that," Moriguchi told me. "Still nobody knows why."

Our next port of call was the site of the villa to which Omura Sumitada retired in 1585, when he relinquished power to his son. The foundations of the modest building are still evident, and with its nearby stream and hillside setting it must have been a comfortable retirement. Pottery from Southeast Asia unearthed here speaks of foreign contacts. An information board credited Sumitada with sponsoring the Four Envoys and promoting ties with Europe, but it omitted any mention of the controversies surrounding him: that his conversion was motivated by political gain; that he gave Nagasaki away to foreigners; and that in his eagerness to please the Jesuits he wreaked destruction on existing religions.

After coming to power in 1550, Sumitada found himself in a vulnerable position, both internally and externally. As an adopted child, he faced rivalry from the natural son of his father, and in 1565 there was a coup attempt. At the same time, his small domain was surrounded by powerful neighbors, who looked on it as easy prey. His survival was facilitated by the link with the Jesuits, which enabled him to obtain Portuguese guns, and in 1563 he was baptised as Dom Bartholomeu. He took to his new religion with the zeal of a convert, wearing a cross and pressing the rest of his domain to join the new faith. People were ordered to convert or go into exile, and Frois writes of how a group of Jesuits accompanied by an armed guard went around supervising the destruction of pagan idols and places of worship. In just seven months over 20,000 people were converted, including Buddhist monks from sixty different temples. (This was happening, ironically, at the very time when Protestant countries like Switzerland, Holland and England were busy destroying Catholic images in Europe.) Frois tells a story of how Sumitada was once on his way to do battle with his enemies when he passed a statue of a war deity:

> Now the idol had above it a cockerel. As the daimyo came there with his squadron, he had his men stop and ordered them to take the idol and burn it, together with the whole temple; and he took the cockerel and gave it a blow with his sword, saying to it, "Oh, how many times have you betrayed me!" And after everything had burned down, he had a very beautiful cross erected on the same spot, and after he and his men had paid very deep reverence to it, they continued on their way to the wars.

The forced transformation of a pagan site is familiar from European history, but in this case there's an extra dimension, for the cockerel is honored in Japanese mythology as a herald of Amaterasu, the sun goddess, whom it wakes each daybreak. Some say too it is the bird referred to in the "bird's roost" (*tori-i*) that stands at the entrance to Shinto shrines. The episode can thus be seen as symbolic of the way Christianity confronted

Japanese values, for in putting the cockerel to the sword Sumitada was negating the native tradition.

At his death, two years into his retirement, Sumitada left behind a distinctive domain. The more than 20,000 converts were served by just four Jesuit padres and nine brothers, indicative of how stretched the resources of the mission were in face of the mass conversions. Ordinary converts had little contact with a priest; most could make confession only once a year at best, and few were able to receive the Eucharist. It makes it all the more surprising that the domain should become a center for Hidden Christians.

The Tokugawa age

A year after Sumitada's death came that of Hideyoshi, following which a power struggle took place that led to the biggest battle in Japanese history at Sekigahara (1600). The portly Tokugawa Ieyasu (1543–1616) emerged as the country's new strongman. He proved the founding father of a remarkable dynasty, which was to rule Japan for the next 268 years. Known as the third great unifier of the country, he built on the work done by his two predecessors: Nobunaga broke the eggs, it is said; Hideyoshi cooked them; but it was Ieyasu who was able to eat them. He had fought as an ally with his two predecessors, but all the time he remained alive to his own interests. Well-known haiku illustrate the difference between the three men: "If the cuckoo won't sing, then I'll kill it," says the brutal Nobunaga. "If the cuckoo won't sing, then I'll make it," says the resourceful Hideyoshi. "If the cuckoo won't sing, then I'll wait till it does," says the ever-patient Ieyasu.

For George Sansom, Ieyasu was "a man of broad mind and calm judgment." Like his predecessors, he took a keen interest in foreigners and the outside world. In the early years of his rule, he continued Hideyoshi's cautious toleration of Christianity in order to maintain the valuable trade links. Churches were rebuilt, and steps were taken to start a cathedral in flourishing Nagasaki. Yet at the same time Ieyasu was wary of threats to his power, and he gave orders that no more daimyo should be baptised. Matters were complicated by the arrival of the Dutch and the English on the one hand, and by Benedictine and Augustinian monks on the other. Both served to undermine the Jesuit position, the former by their hostility and the latter by their rivalry. In addition, Japan had built up a fleet of Red Seal ships with a patent to trade abroad, and it was steadily developing its trade with Manila. It all meant that the Jesuit link with Macao was losing its glitter, as step by step the monopoly of the Great Ship was eroded.

It was in these years that the English pilot William Adams rose to prominence (he was the model for James Clavell's protagonist in the novel *Shogun*, published in 1975). He had arrived in 1600 shortly before the Battle of Sekigahara, and was interviewed in Osaka Castle by Ieyasu who saw his potential in terms of skills and knowledge. In the years that followed, the Englishman showed how to build ships in the European style and became a trusted confidant of the Japanese leader. The picture he painted of the Jesuits was colored by his background, for he had grown up in an England ever fearful of Catholic plots. The Iberians were after more than the conquest of souls, he insisted; they were after the conquest of the country.

The early years of the new age proved eventful for the Omura domain. Sumitada's son and successor, Omura Yoshiaki (1568–1615), had been brought up by the Jesuits as Dom Sancho but severed relations with them in 1605. In the next year he converted to Nichiren Buddhism. "Why?" I asked Moriguchi.

"Politics," he answered. "He didn't fight with Ieyasu at Sekigahara and stayed neutral, so his position was weak. Tokugawa allies wanted his land. Actually he resigned and made his son daimyo, but it was just a kind of tactic to keep power. Ieyasu didn't like daimyo to be Christian, and that was bad for him.

So he decided to join the religion of his friend, the daimyo of Kumamoto, and become stronger that way. That's why he founded this temple," he added.

Before us stood Honkyo-ji, a temple founded by Yoshiaki in 1608. It was built on the site of a demolished church and stood beside the main pathway in these parts, the Nagasaki Kaido. The temple has an exaggeratedly long wall to suggest it is bigger than its size, for it was an advertisement to the world at large that Yoshiaki was no Christian.

"Look over there," Moriguchi said, pointing through the graveyard. "That was where the Nagasaki Kaido used to run. The temple was a kind of showcase. Everyone who came past here, all the important people, would know that this was the Nichiren temple of Yoshiaki. And look at the graveyard: can you see the big tomb? It's Yoshiaki's. It's very high, isn't it? It's so everyone could see it from outside."

The tomb was almost comical in its vertical elongation, like someone in a group photo trying to catch attention by standing on tiptoe. Yoshiaki's change of faith was followed up even more aggressively by his son, also baptised as a baby, who became a vigorous anti-Christian. It was a policy that enabled his descendants to stay in power until the abolition of the feudal system in early Meiji times, and the small graveyard was full of carefully numbered tombs indicating family rulers. But where was the grave of Sumitada, I wondered? "It's a mystery," Moriguchi said. "We know he was buried in a church, but the church was destroyed. No one knows what happened to the grave. The Omura Historical Committee is investigating that."

The path to persecution

Although Ieyasu had started out with toleration of Christianity, by the end of the decade his patience with the Catholics was wearing thin. After asking Manila for help with building Japan's trading fleet, he was dismayed to find that the Spanish exploited the opportunity to deliver missionaries. Then in 1609 friction developed with Macao following the execution of Japanese there for causing a disturbance. In retaliation Ieyasu ordered a Portuguese ship named *Madre de Deus* to be seized, the captain of which chose to sink it following a three-day battle. Thereafter, Portuguese ships were restricted to Nagasaki. Meanwhile, the Dutch were granted a license to trade at Hirado, and in 1611 Ieyasu appointed William Adams instead of the Jesuit Joao Rodrigues as his official interpreter. The Portuguese priest had been a major player in Japanese affairs, for he negotiated matters of state while acting as commercial agent for the Jesuits. In his place Adams used his position to feed the shogun stories of Catholic intrigue. So influential was the Englishman that in later years a Jesuit report was to blame him for single-handedly wrecking their mission.

In 1612 there was a bribery scandal involving two Christians, one of whom was a daimyo and the other a member of Ieyasu's council. It suggested that ties between believers were stronger than allegiance to the shogunate. Word also reached Ieyasu that at the execution of a Christian, a priest had told the assembled crowd that obedience to the Church should override obedience to the daimyo. It prompted the Japanese leader to take action, and Christianity was banned altogether in shogunal domains. Other daimyo followed suit, some to curry favor and some out of hostility to the religion.

Two years later came an epoch-making proclamation, known as the Statement on the Expulsion of the Bateren, which marked a decisive turning point. The edict was drafted by a Zen monk named Konchiin Suden and began, interestingly, with the declaration that "Japan is the Land of the Gods." There followed familiar charges: that missionaries were seeking to colonize Japan; that they destroyed native practices; and that their religion subverted Japanese customs. In short it was a pernicious doctrine. Foreign missionaries were ordered to leave at once and Japanese converts to give up the faith. In the period that followed, churches were destroyed. Jesuit buildings demolished and there were exemplary punishments in urban centers. In Kyoto, where some 7,000 Christians were concentrated in Dios-machi (God's Town), people were bundled up in straw sacks on the banks of the River Kamo and left until they apostatized.

The anti-Christian moves came at a time of rising tension between the Tokugawa regime and supporters of Toyotomi Hideyori, son of Hideyoshi. Ieyasu had been made a guardian of the child, and though he had seized power for himself at the Battle of Sekigahara, he let Hideyori grow up in his father's castle. As the boy matured, he became a focal point for the disaffected, including Christians, and in 1614 Ieyasu felt compelled to lay siege to the castle. There were missionaries within its walls, and among the emblems of the defenders were Christian symbols, some of which provocatively displayed the patron saint of Spain and the slogan "Great Protector." Facing them was a massive army of 155,000 attackers, led by the seventy-four-year-old Ieyasu. So well had the castle defenses been set up—the moats were seventy to ninety yards wide and the walls twenty yards high—that the summer siege proved ineffective. Unable to make a breakthrough, the wily Ieyasu withdrew and negotiated a truce by means of which he induced his opponents to fill in part of the moat. It meant that when he treacherously resumed the siege in the winter of 1615, he was soon able to overrun the defense. For the Catholics, it was a disaster.

Although most of the missionaries had left the country following the expulsion order, it's thought that up to forty-seven of them went underground and were shielded by sympathizers. These rebel priests lived in safe houses, held Mass in secret, and only emerged in the anonymity of darkness. Protected by an underground organization, they moved from house to house to escape detection. Some were concealed beneath floorboards or secreted behind toilets, reminiscent of the "priest holes" in English stately homes. In this way, the missionaries not only managed to serve the needs of practitioners but even had some success in proselytizing. Over the next twelve years, the Jesuits alone claimed 17,000 baptisms. Meanwhile, other priests slipped into the country aboard the China Ship, managing to sneak ashore amid the confusion of its arrival. Alarmed by the developments, Tokugawa Hidetada (1579–1632), who had taken over power from his father, initiated a more brutal persecution. Less secure than Ieyasu, the new shogun was nervous of foreign aggression and in 1616 issued orders that anyone even suspected of shielding Christians should be put to death.

One of the priests to reenter Japan in these years was a local man, Thomas Tsuji (1570–1627), described by Moriguchi as a master of disguise. Born into the Omura nobility, he was educated by the Jesuits and entered the order in 1589, becoming one of the first Japanese priests. Following his expulsion in 1614, he went to Macao, where he remained for four years before returning to Japan in the guise of a merchant. While European missionaries avoided going out in daytime for obvious reasons, Tsuji was able to move around freely. His favorite role was that of a wood seller, which enabled him to knock on doors without suspicion. Once, however, while he was celebrating Mass in a private house soldiers burst in and arrested him. Held in Omura for thirteen months, he was sent with others to be burned at the stake in Nagasaki.

There were other incidents involving missionaries in these years. In 1617 two priests, one Jesuit and one Franciscan, sought to provoke the authorities by defying the ban on preaching. One of them, Father Jean-Baptiste Machado, had yearned for martyrdom since the age of ten and, brought before the daimyo, he surprised him by saying that far from fearing death he would gladly be dismembered in Japanese fashion. It took three blows to sever his neck, after the first two of which he is said to have given thanks to God. Together with his fellow missionary, he was buried in a common grave, which became a focus for devotion for the local Christians. As with the 26 Martyrs, rather than intimidating the faithful the executions served only to deepen their faith.

Impressed by the positive effect of the martyrdom, two other priests decided to follow suit. One of them, Father Alphonso, declared publicly that he did not recognize the ruler of Japan, but only the ruler of heaven. To the authorities it was proof positive of the religion's subversive nature, and the men were executed. This time the daimyo ordered the bodies to be thrown into the sea with rocks around their necks so that there would be no remains. Nonetheless the martyrdom proved effective, for according to Richard Cocks, in charge of the English trading post in Hirado, it made the Omura Christians think how best to follow their example.

"Have you heard of Suzuta Prison?" Moriguchi asked me. "It's not far from here. Thirty-five Christians were kept in a room, very small. That room was only sixteen feet wide and twenty-four feet long. There wasn't even room to lie down. Unbelievable. Maybe you can't imagine. Some of them were held there for as long as five years. They couldn't go outside, and the toilet was in a corner."

The persecutions were part of a national campaign, for the Tokugawa had initiated a series of anti-Christian moves that grew increasingly severe. Oddly, the situation paralleled that of Europe, where the Catholic Church was itself turning the screw on its enemies (Galileo was put on trial in 1633). Yet despite the notoriety of the Inquisition, the Japanese persecution was even more drastic. According to one estimate, between 1540 and 1794 the Portuguese Inquisition led to the burning of 1,175 persons. In Britain over a similar time frame, almost 1,000 people were persecuted for witchcraft. By comparison, the Japanese executed over 4,000 people in just thirty years, with countless thousands of others tortured, ruined or exiled.

Intensification

The coming to power in 1623 of Iemitsu, the third Tokugawa shogun, brought a more systematic approach to the anti-Christian measures. A temperamental type, he was as wily as he was willful, and, according to Anesaki Masaharu, he was "eager to suppress and exterminate anything and everything that resisted his high command." Opinions about him range from sadistic to paranoid, and on several occasions he is known to have attended interrogations of Christians. The religion posed a threat to his personal philosophy, for he deified his grandfather Ieyasu as founding father of the shogunate and built a mausoleum for him at the Toshogu Shrine in Nikko that remains one of Japan's most spectacular sights. In this way, he made his own ancestor his god, allegiance to whom would brook no competition from Deusu.

Under Iemitsu, prison, physical punishment and financial incentives were used in an orchestrated campaign against Christianity. In the early years the authorities relied on mass executions to intimidate the local populations. The Great Martyrdom of Kyoto in 1619 involved fifty-two people; that of Edo in 1623 fifty people; and that of Nagasaki in 1632 fifty-five people. The policy proved counterproductive, as, far from dampening religious enthusiasm, the martyrdom fanned the flames of Christian fervor. In 1628 came the first use of *fumie* (standing on a picture), by which people had to tread on religious images as proof of renunciation. (The practice did not become widespread until

1640, with paper used at first, then wood, and finally in 1649 twenty bronze images cast in metal obtained from altars.)

Collective responsibility meant that family members would be punished along with the individual concerned, and groups of households *(goningumi)* were set up for mutual surveillance. In 1635, forced registration with temples was introduced, with supervision by priests. It meant that every single Japanese citizen was obliged by law to belong to a Buddhist sect. In 1640, a centralized prosecution office *(shumon aratame yaku)* was set up in Edo, in addition to which each domain had its own bureau. Thus, by the time the country entered the period of isolationism, the religious impulse of the populace was being monitored in almost Big Brother style.

To win the propaganda battle, prosecutors soon came to realize that apostasy was a far greater weapon than martyrdom. Much publicity was given to *korobi Kirishitan* (fallen Christians), and *korobi bateren* (fallen priests) were treated as a major victory. To make believers recant, authorities tried threats, enticements and persuasion, followed by the infliction of pain—pain at its most extreme. "Nearly every form of torture was used that human ingenuity and savagery could devise," writes Ivan Morris. There is virtually nothing one can think of that wasn't tried— water torture, snake pits, branding, slicing open with a bamboo saw, amputation, roasting alive, crushing limbs, suffocation through overcrowding, suspension upside down, even being tied to stakes in shallow sea water to be slowly drowned by the incoming tide. In public burnings, fires were lit just far enough from victims so as to scorch the skin without the release of a swift death. Worst of all was "the pit," of which the historian C. R. Boxer has left a graphic description:

> The victim was tightly bound around the body as high
> as the breast (one hand being left free to give the signal

of recantation) and then hung downwards from a gallows into a pit, which usually contained excreta and other filth, the top of the pit being level with his knees. In order to give the blood some vent, the forehead was highly slashed with a knife. Some of the stronger martyrs lived for more than a week in this position, but the majority did not survive more than a day or two.

Not surprisingly, given the consequences, there was a sharp drop in the number of Christians. In 1612 there were over 300,000; by 1625 there were half or fewer. Some fled abroad, and Japanese communities sprang up in Manila, Burma and Cambodia. Those who remained in the country tried to conceal their religion: the majority lived in remote areas where the arm of the authorities did not extend so readily, though the citizens of Nagasaki remained a hard core. Another consequence was that the number of missionaries volunteering for Japan dropped off, for the agonies of torture held less appeal than the glories of martyrdom. Paradise was the vision, not hell on earth.

In the 1630s a series of edicts brought increasingly tighter restrictions on foreign contacts, some of which were specifically aimed at Christians. The first edict in 1633 stipulated rewards for the whereabouts of priests and the searching of foreign ships. Suspected Christians had to sign an oath of apostasy to escape punishment, and one example, signed by thirty-nine Omura people, is intriguing for the way the public pledge is made to the very God it renounces:

> We were Kirishitan for many years. Yet we found out
> the Kirishitan religion is an evil religion. It regards
> the afterlife as the most important. They teach that
> those who disobey the padre's orders will be excom-
> municated and be cast into Inferno . . . but the padres

> are plotting to take the lands of others. . . . Hereafter
> we shall never revoke our apostasy, not even entertain
> the slightest thought thereof. . . . There is no false-
> hood in this respect. If there is, let us be punished by
> the Father, Son and Holy Ghost, as well as by Mother
> Mary and all angels and saints.

The last of the anti-foreign edicts, which came out in 1639, banned Portuguese ships altogether, and in Tokugawa records the reason was ascribed to the smuggling of missionaries into the country. At the same time, Japanese who had gone abroad were banned from re-entering the country, as if Christianity was a contagious disease to which they might have been exposed. The laws were accompanied by anti-Christian propaganda in which Jesuits were depicted as evil villains, willing to bribe and deceive in their attempt to contaminate souls. The combined effect was devastating for the church. As Japan moved into an age of isolation, the last surviving missionary, Brother Konishi Mancio, was put to death in 1644. The Christian community had been broken, its leaders wiped out, and even the most stubborn of adherents cowed into submission. Or so it seemed.

The Kohri case

Amazingly, despite the severity of the persecution, pockets of believers continued to practice in secret. One such group was discovered in 1657 in the village of Kohri, on the fringe of Omura City. A total of 608 believers in all were arrested, and after interrogation 197 recanted and the rest were condemned to death. To exploit the propaganda effect, they were divided into groups, some of whom were sent to be executed in the former Christian hotspots of Nagasaki, Hirado and Shimabara. Those who remained numbered 131, who were condemned to be beheaded.

Moriguchi took me to the Parting Rock, where they were allowed to take leave of their families. No moss has ever grown on the rock, he said, because of the saltiness of the tears shed. We then drove to the execution site, where a monument stands in a forlorn plot of grass hemmed in on both sides by cheap timber-clad housing. It was a surprisingly banal scene, somehow disconnected from the gruesome events of the past. One side of the monument showed an angel passing a branch to a peasant about to be executed, which reminded me of the *sakaki* branch used in Shinto as an offering to the *kami*. I asked Moriguchi about it, thinking it may have local significance, but his pained expression and sharp intake of breath told me he did not know either. "*Sumimasen*," he said assuming responsibility, "I'll check with the Omura Historical Committee."

Afterwards we drove to the burial site of the Christians, passing on the way the section of the Nagasaki Kaido pathway where for twenty days the executed heads had been displayed. Walking between severed heads is a macabre thought, though the folks of Edo times were used to such things. Summary execution was normal practice, even for trivial crimes, and the sight of corpses was commonplace. They were used by samurai to test the sharpness of their swords, and bodies were sometimes piled up to five high to see if swords would cut through the layered navels. Francesco Carletti reported seeing a lord sever a body in half and then calmly inspect the blade to make sure it had suffered no damage (the sword's value was judged accordingly). Afterwards, his followers tested their own swords on different parts of the body, leaving chunks of human flesh scattered all over the ground. "The whole thing is carried out as a pastime, without turning a hair, very much as with us the anatomy of dead bodies is carried out in the interests of medical science," he concludes.

The Kohri Christians were buried at two different locations in the village, some 500 yards apart. One mound, known as

Kubizuka, was for heads only, and the other, called Douzuka, was for the decapitated trunks. Christianity was a religion of resurrection, and rumor had it that if the body parts were buried together, the victims would be able to magically unite and return to life. The mounds are surrounded now by suburban housing, which struck me as odd given the Japanese belief in restless spirits. I would have imagined the graves to be fearful places, and asked Moriguchi about it. "Perhaps the spirits were not restless," he said after some thought; "perhaps they found the salvation they sought."

Martyrdom

I came away from Omura filled with images of persecution, and on the train back to Nagasaki pondered the whole matter of martyrdom. The 4,000 or so known to have died for their faith include 71 Europeans, but the overwhelming majority were ordinary Japanese from the lower strata of society. Countless others disappeared, or were banished, or died later of injuries. What had made folk like the Kohri villagers cling so tightly to their faith? They would have been born and raised Catholic just as their parents, for they represented the third generation of converts. But was that enough to explain the willingness to accept martyrdom? It seemed there was something else at work, something more than just individual faith, as if villagers were sustained by the collective strength of the group. Endo Shusaku had written about it:

> It has been my long-held supposition that because the sense of community, based on blood relationships, was so much stronger among villagers in those days, it was not left up to individuals to determine whether they would endure persecution or succumb. Instead this matter was decided by the village as a whole. . . .

That I felt was the fundamental distinction between
Japanese Christian communities and the martyrs in
foreign lands.

The early Christian Tertullian famously wrote that "the
blood of the martyrs is the seed of the Church," and Catholic
orthodoxy was keen to promote the propaganda value of martyrdom. Jesuit publications such as *Instructions on Martyrdom* and
Exhortations to Martyrdom were widely circulated. Their gist was
that eternal salvation outweighed the mere temporary nature of
physical distress: better to suffer a few hours of extreme pain than
to endure the horrors of hell for all eternity. The writings argued
with intellectual rigor for the need to accept death when faced
with an implacable foe, and that those who remained faithful
would be imbued with God's grace to resist even the worst of
tortures. Preparation for martyrdom was carefully spelled out:
confessing one's sins; forgiving one's persecutors; prayers to fortify
the inner soul; visualization of Jesus and the coming of angels;
and a final word of benefit to onlookers—"There is no greater
joy than this, because it is the way to eternal bliss," for example.

Death must necessarily be met once in your life, you
cannot know how and when it will come, even if you
escape it this time. Think that it is Deus' special favor
and that you can thus face death in preparedness,
and meet it as your sacrifice in repentance, then your
death will certainly be received as an act of redemp-
tion, a work of great merit.

Excuses for avoiding martyrdom were also dealt with in systematic manner. Attachment to material things; attachment to
family and friends; obedience to one's superior; fear of torture
and death—all are mercilessly rejected. "Those who having been

instructed in the way of Truth fall from it will be more bitterly afflicted in Inferno than those who have never come into contact with the Law," runs a grave warning. The rules of acceptable behavior were meticulous in their detail. Moving house and concealing one's religion were all right. So was not speaking up. But denial of one's religion was a grave sin, and there was a stark warning for those thinking of becoming Hidden Christians while publicly denying their faith.

> One might say: My mind is not changed at all but I have declared apostasy only in appearance, for continuing to live. This is an evident fraud. It is usual with a traitor that he says otherwise than as he thinks. How could one be released from punishment and be saved through a pretext like this? The offense of apostasy and the punishment due to it remain the same, regardless of whether it be real or only in disguise. Listen to what Jesus said on this point: one who shall deny me before men, him shall I declare before Deus Padre to be a stranger to me. He says again: No one can serve two lords, to respect one means to deny the other. . . . Thus an apostate, if not real, is working to discredit the religion and disgrace the noble name of Jesus, and the crime is never to be pardoned.

Underlying such arguments are the vital concepts of heaven and hell. These are so compelling that even in the present scientific age, according to *Newsweek*'s religious correspondent, Lisa Miller, 81 percent of Americans and 51 percent of British believe in them. Her book *Heaven: Our Enduring Fascination with the Afterlife* (2010) traces the European tradition back to 165 BCE, when a Jew called Daniel got the inspiration to insert human souls into a place previously reserved for divinities. The idea captured the imagination of others and quickly spread like wildfire. Now it is such an embedded part of the culture that it seems a natural part of our mental landscape.

Given the brutality of the persecution, the stoicism with which Japanese approached death struck Europeans of the age as remarkable. "They race to martyrdom as if to a festival," wrote Father Organtino. "There is no nation on earth that fears death less," commented Francesco Carletti. It makes one wonder if there was a cultural component. For Joao Rodriques, who noted the way in which Japanese calmly ate and drank before ritual suicide, it was linked to the sense of honor. Others, however, have tied the stoical attitude to suppression of the ego. In *The Japanese Mind*, Kishimoto Hideo argues that awareness of evanescence is such a fundamental component of the Buddhist worldview that, "For the Japanese death is within life." Ritualized and codified, the thinking became part of Bushido: "The way of the samurai is to be found in death," famously proclaimed the eighteenth-century *Hagakure*. Cherry blossom, samurai, seppuku—the Japanese preoccupation with death has a long tradition.

"When you get to the roots of the Japanese soul, I think they are embodied in the kamikaze pilots," said the film director Taku Shinjo in an interview. He's not the only one to have made such a claim. Is there a connection with martyrdom? Does the readiness for death typify traits of the culture, such as the subjugation of self? The ideology of martyrdom, as that of the kamikaze, urged the achievement of posthumous glory. For Christians the reward would be in heaven; for the kamikaze it was joining the *kami* at Yasukuni Shrine. In both cases the sacrifice of life would serve the larger cause of church or state, and the hero-martyr would achieve immortality in the memory of others. In this way individual death was transcended for the greater good.

Many of the most touching stories of martyrdom concern children, for under Japanese justice, with its collectivist mindset, it was common practice for the whole family to be punished. An egregious example is the only known pregnant martyr in Catholic history, Hashimoto Tecla, who was executed along with five of her children in 1619. Part of a group of fifty-two, they were tied to stakes on the banks of the Kamogawa in Kyoto: Tecla was accompanied on one side by a child of twelve, on the other by a child of eight, and her three-year-old daughter was tied to her chest. The Englishman Richard Cocks witnessed the event and was astonished by the fortitude, for even as the flames rose he noted that the children did not forsake their faith. When Tecla's corpse was found, it was fused together with her youngest daughter. (They were part of the 188 people beatified by the Catholic Church in 2008.)

Cruelty

In light of the above, the question arises as to why the authorities were so virulent in their persecution? Why should it matter so much to them what a person believed? Fear of colonization was a major factor, as we have seen. "The shogun and his Governors in their hearts cleave to the notion that the law of God is a design and device for the conquest of kingdoms," said a Jesuit report of 1621. But there was something more, it seems to me, something in Christianity that was inimical to Japanese values. Take suicide, for instance, an act of the highest virtue for a samurai but a sin for Christians. There was too the vexing issue of allegiance. "Socially, Christianity was inconsistent with the feudal hierarchy, and ethically it was opposed to the code of the warrior class" is how George Sansom sums it all up.

An incident involving a samurai called Zensho Shichiemon illustrates the point. Though Christianity was forbidden on pain of death, he chose to convert and even the priest who baptised him warned of the dire consequences. When brought before his daimyo, he remained adamant in his refusal to recant. "I would obey in any other matter," he declared, "but I cannot accept any order that is opposed to my eternal salvation." He was beheaded, just four months after his baptism; loyalty to a heavenly lord had overridden loyalty to his worldly lord. Feudal loyalty was given special emphasis under Tokugawa neo-Confucianism, in which allegiance to one's superior was made into a supreme virtue. In this clash of Christian and Confucian, there could be little room for compromise.

But what of the cruelty? What had driven the authorities to use such horrendous means of torture? The extremities of the Japanese reception of Christianity were also noted by George Sansom: "Nowhere else in Asia were Christian propagandists able to gain such a ready hearing for the gospel from all classes and nowhere were they more kindly treated. Yet nowhere were they more savagely repressed. This paradox is to be explained by the dual nature of Japanese society, which combined a strong sense of social ethics with a great ruthlessness in the enforcement of law."

One can't help speculating on how far there was a cultural aspect involved. Even today, Japanese prisons and death row facilities are notorious for their inhumanity, and though I've been often struck by the kindness of Japanese people, I've been equally shocked by the callousness towards animal suffering. Was there an ability to disassociate from those in an out-group? Perhaps meticulousness also played a part, for the zeal of the torturers was matched by the fervor of believers. Scourging provides an example. Even missionaries were astonished by the severity with which Japanese took to the practice, with the result that church floors were sometimes splattered with blood.

It's well to remember the nature of the age, however, and that equally cruel acts were being inflicted in Europe in these times. Torture was common in Elizabethan interrogations, and one form of punishment involved partially strangulating victims by hanging them, then drawing them behind a vehicle while still conscious before slicing open their stomach (in extreme cases, their genitalia) and cutting them into quarters.

I was mulling over such morbid thoughts when a telephone call came through on my mobile phone. It was Moriguchi-san, who was ringing to tell me he'd learned there were two Catholic churches in the city, with 2,200 members. Twenty-two hundred out of a population of 80,000—it didn't seem much in the light of all the sacrifices made. He also told me that he had contacted the Omura Historical Committee and identified from which tree the branch had been taken that we saw in the monument we visited. It was a palm. Of course! The Roman symbol of victory had been adapted by early Christians to signify the conquest of the spirit over death. Moriguchi had come up trumps, and it was one reason I liked Japan so much. You could always rely on taxi drivers!

Chapter Seven

Apocalypse
(Shimabara)

Hot water

One of the confusions that arise when living in Japan is that place names can often be misleading. It's odd, for instance, to hear that Kyoto has a nice coastline when the city is about as far from the sea as it's possible to get. The confusion is of city and prefecture, which go by the same name. Something similar is at play with the famous Shimabara Uprising of 1637, for one might have thought it to center on Shimabara City, or Shimabara Castle. In fact the main events took place at Hara Castle some way to the south, and the uprising takes its name from the Shimabara peninsula. It lies in the eastern part of Nagasaki prefecture, and it was there that one of the bloodiest events in Japanese history took place.

From Nagasaki the road to Shimabara leads through the volcanic national park of Unzen, where there is a mountain peak that only appeared in 1991 following an eruption that killed forty-three people. It goes by the no-nonsense name of Heisei Shinzan—New Mountain of Heisei Era. The road runs along an attractive coastline of layered hills, as in a Chinese ink painting, till one comes to the town of Obama where the steam rising out of roadside gutters announces that one has entered a hot spring area. From here the road turns inland and upwards, past steeply terraced fields and fertile valleys. There's a small Buddhist theme park dominated by a larger-than-life *tengu*, as if the legendary long-nosed monster was a bodhisattva. A few sharp curves later and the bus deposits one at Unzen Hell—a desolate hillside area of scorched rocks and billowing steam. It was here that a horrifying form of torture was carried out in the years of persecution, when Christians were scalded in the sulfuric water.

The idea of using Unzen Hell to force recantation was hit upon by prosecutors in the late 1620s. There were two methods: application to parts of the body, and total immersion (illustrations show people being pushed off a cliff). Between 1627 and 1633 thirty-three people were killed and sixty others tortured here. It's a gruesome thought as you wander around the steaming rocks and gurgling vents. At one point a thick blanket of warm steam enshrouded me, from out of which I emerged to find myself at Screaming Hell, so-called because the roar resembles that of the dead as they descend into the Buddhist inferno. The temperature of the water here reaches 120 degrees, and the steam rises a hundred or more feet into the air. When Endo Shusaku visited, the writer wondered how long he would manage to hold out if subjected to the torture. Aware of his weakness, he presumed he would lose consciousness at the very prospect. I had similar feelings.

Somewhere I had read that there was a small memorial to the torture victims, and while searching for it I was reminded again of how marginal Christian matters are in the flow of Japanese history. Signboards made no mention of them, preferring to concentrate on the flora and fauna that—remarkably—flourish in such surrounds. Instead, the area has been jointly claimed by Buddhism and Shinto in the complementary manner that characterizes Japanese syncretism. At one entrance to the park stands Onsen Jinja (Hot Spring Shrine), in response to the sense of awe that the springs evoke. At the other entrance is a collection of weathered Jizo (the bodhisattva guardian of lost souls), ready to guide the dead over the riverbed that separates the land of the living from the Buddhist afterworld.

Shimabara Castle

From Unzen the bus crosses the peninsula to Shimabara City, dominated by a splendid castle with pristine white walls atop a stone foundation. Rebuilt in modern times (the main keep is in ferroconcrete), it had first been established between 1618 and 1624 by Matsukura Shigemasa, a man whose name is besmirched with the kind of infamy attached to the Sheriff of Nottingham in the Robin Hood legends—both were cruel tyrants who squeezed the last drop out of the local peasantry. Given the domain as a reward for services to the Tokugawa, the Japanese daimyo built a castle way above his station and beyond his means. To compensate, he taxed everything he could. There were levies on heating, on windows, on shelves, on entrances. There was a tax for being born, and another for dying. Should any poor wretch be incapable of coughing up, the punishments were severe: some were thrown into water-filled rooms to rot, while others were hung upside down. Wives and children were taken hostage and mistreated. Worst of all was the infamous *mino odori* (raincoat dance), in which victims were wrapped in a straw jacket, doused in lamp oil and set alight. As they leapt about in agony, onlookers laughed derisively at the "dance" they were performing. Cruel times, indeed.

The area had had Christian connections since 1563, when the Portuguese Jesuit Luis de Almeida (1525–84) visited from Omura. He had arrived in Japan as a merchant with some medical knowledge, and only subsequently joined the Jesuits, with whom he was able to use his healing skills to win over converts.

Progress was furthered by the daimyo, Arima Harunobu (1567–1612), who had been baptised at a young age and who used his Portuguese connections to obtain guns and ward off a powerful enemy. In his efforts to create a Christian realm, Harunobu is said to have destroyed more than forty Buddhist temples and Shinto shrines. In 1576, 20,000 of the domain's citizens were baptised in just six months.

After the expulsion edict of 1587, Jesuits fled to the Arima domain for safety, and at one time there were as many as seventy missionaries, with an equal number of churches. It became a model for how the Jesuits hoped the rest of Japan would develop. There was a flourishing seminary where not only theology but European arts were taught, and among the first batch of graduates were the Four Envoys who were sent by Valignano to Rome. A later graduate, Peter Kibe (1587–1639) became the first Japanese to visit Jerusalem, after an epic journey in which he walked overland from India and joined a caravan to cross the Arabian desert.

In 1600 at the Battle of Sekigahara, Arima Harunobu sided with the Tokugawa forces, which ensured his survival under the new regime. However, he was caught up in the corruption scandal of 1610 when a fellow Christian promised to get him extra territory, and in the aftermath the daimyo was stripped of his domain and ordered to commit seppuku. Like others of his faith, he refused on religious grounds and had a follower behead him instead. The domain was subsequently awarded to Matsukura Shigemasa, who was keen to prove his loyalty to the shogun by the zeal with which he persecuted Christians. He set up a new capital in the north of the domain, but the religion remained firmly rooted in the south, and even as late as 1632 there were five missionaries active in the area.

At Shimabara Castle, a Kirishitan Museum houses relics from the past. There are swords and flanges bearing crosses, from an era when their owners felt bold enough to display them openly. Other exhibits, such as a small icon concealed within a bamboo pole, show the furtive nature of the practice as the persecution intensified. The Maria Kannon is the prime example. In appearance it is simply a Buddhist statue showing the deity of compassion. Though supposedly sexless, Kannon is often depicted with graceful curves and a feminine air: despite having started life in India as a male, the deity had somewhere on the long journey through China undergone a sex change. To signify her limitless compassion, it's not unusual in Japan to see a motherly Kannon carrying a child. For Japanese Christians, it was but a short step to identification with Maria (the name taught them by Spanish and Portuguese priests).

The cult of the Madonna was already strong among southern Catholics in Europe, and for Hidden Christians she became a central focus of worship. The Maria Kannon were sometimes marked with a surreptitious cross on the back or base, but as often as not they simply consisted of a feminine figure. Thoughts apparently directed towards the Pure Land were secretly focused on the crucifixion. The statues thus resonate with a powerful duality: revealed and concealed; open and hidden; East and West.

Outside Shimabara Castle stands an unusual Catholic church, and I wandered over to look around. It has a striking design, with a high arch and circular layout as if to show that modern architecture too can be attractive. The stained-glass windows tell the history of the region, from the coming of Almeida to the persecutions at Unzen, and at the entrance stands the statue of a youth with the middle fingers of his hands missing. "In the eyes of the authorities," says the accompanying sign, "the Christians were less than animals and so deserved fewer fingers than animals." It's a striking example of the dangers of dehumanization. Turn your enemies into insects, and you can crush them without pity. Or better still, think of them as pieces of wood, and you can carry out inhumane experiments like the infamous Japanese Unit 731 in World War Two.

Hara Castle

By the 1630s, the Shimabara populace had suffered more than they could stand. For several years in a row the crops failed because of drought, and there was widespread famine. Yet still the overtaxation continued. "Even Japanese human nature, accustomed for ages to subordination and submission, could stand it no longer," writes W. E. Griffis. The region was ready to explode, and the spark to set it off came when the pregnant wife of a farmer was assaulted by a bailiff. The village reacted in rage, and like a bush fire the conflagration spread throughout the region. All of a sudden there was a full-scale uprising, and rebels marched on Shimabara Castle, though they were unable to breach the defenses. In the nearby Amakusa Islands, where conditions were equally harsh, a similar uprising took place. Following talks, the rebel groups decided to converge at Hara Castle in the south of the peninsula, since its coastal location offered a natural fortress. It had been vacated following a "one-castle, one-domain" law introduced by the Tokugawa, and though the buildings were destroyed, the moats and embankments were still in place.

Today, the castle lies peaceful and grassy on the shores of the Ariake Sea. It stands on a small promontory that ends with a hundred-foot cliff, and the concentric defensive positions spread inland, amounting to a total circumference of two miles. At the top is an area of flat land that commands views over the surrounding sea, while along the peninsula the mountains at Unzen are clearly visible. Day-trippers and families wander about, much as at a National Trust site in Britain, and I stood for a while trying to imagine the scene four hundred years earlier. The ringleaders would have gathered here at the top, a small group of

Christian samurai who had become masterless when their lords were dispossessed. For a leader they had turned to a sixteen-year-old known as Amakusa Shiro, and a huge statue of him as a robust youth with a visionary gaze dominates the grounds.

Around the top, the rebels were arranged by village, each under the charge of its headman. Less than a third were fighting men, with the rest made up of wives, children and the elderly. As farmers and fishermen, the villagers were untrained in fighting and for weapons used anything they could get their hands on: swords, scythes, spears—even sticks and stones. You'd hardly think they would have a chance against well-armed shogunate troops, yet, though they were outnumbered, they managed to hold out for almost three months. They even scored some early victories, for the enemy was disorganized, badly led and fraught with factional friction (troops were drawn from different domains). In response, the shogunate installed a new leader and drew on reinforcements until they had a massive 120,000 in all, more even than the winning army at Sekigahara. Among them is thought to have been the legendary swordsman Miyamoto Musashi (c.1584–1645), acting in an advisory role. The new policy was to bide time and starve the rebels into submission.

The siege took place in the midst of winter, and exposure killed off many on both sides. Negotiations were carried out by letters, which were attached to arrows and fired into the enemy's territory. The attacking general promised to spare the lives of the non-Christians and reduce their land tax; the rebels responded by asserting unity and that they would all be brothers in the hereafter. To apply pressure, the attackers took hostage family members of the rebel leaders and brought them to the fort to urge surrender. At one point a large ship came into view, causing joy among the rebels, who thought it was Portuguese, but to their shock it fired cannon at them. It turned out to be a Dutch ship, requested by the government to help with the assault. Fellow Christians they may have been, but the Protestants had little love for their Catholic enemies, and there was political advantage in supporting the shogun.

The rebels survived at first on the stores they had, but as the siege intensified supplies ran out. A raiding party sent to forage for food was captured, and when their stomachs were cut open it was seen that they had been subsisting on plants and seaweed. Shortly afterwards the final assault was launched, and despite fierce fighting the outer defenses were soon breached. Three days of butchery followed, for orders had been given that not a single defender should be spared. As fires raged around the castle, thousands chose to throw themselves into the flames rather than be slaughtered. Ditches flowed with blood, and the piles of heads (for men) and noses (for women and children) rose ever higher as the victors tallied up the number of victims. It is thought some 37,000 were killed in all. A staggering 10,000 heads were set up on stakes around the perimeter of the castle as a grim warning to others, while another 3,300 heads were sent to Nagasaki to intimidate the populace there. Four heads were even placed on the small bridge leading to the artificial island of Dejima, where the Portuguese were confined.

It's invidious to play the numbers game when it concerns the dead, but the number of those killed at Shimabara is almost identical to the 39,000 who died in the Nagasaki atomic bomb (66,000 died at Hiroshima). Nagasaki and Hiroshima are scoured into the global consciousness as egregious examples of modern warfare, yet there has long been a far more lethal weapon available: human nature. The six-week blood bath of the Nanking Massacre of 1937 is a case in point, dwarfing other atrocities in enormity (over 200,00 according to the International Military Tribunal for the Far East, though the figure is disputed). In terms of devastation, even a nuclear bomb cannot compare with the savagery of the human hand.

It's worth remembering too the cold-blooded savagery that took place in Europe in this age. A religious uprising known as the Prayer Book Rebellion had taken place in southwest England in 1549, following which royalist troops had gone around indiscriminately killing hundreds of defeated participants. A closer equivalent to Shimabara, however, would be the Irish Confederate Wars, for following the rebellion of 1641 Oliver Cromwell's soldiers acted with such ferocious brutality that it's estimated around a quarter of the population lost their lives. In this way, on opposite sides of the globe and at almost the same time, Catholic peasants were being slaughtered wholesale by autocrats who saw them as a threat to their security.

Filled with such grim thoughts, I wandered back to the castle entrance near which are located a handful of graves. One was for Amakusa Shiro, though it's purely symbolic and contains no remains. On the day of the battle a row had taken place about who could claim his death, and to identify his corpse his mother was brought to the site. Unwilling to help her son's enemy, she inadvertently identified the body by bursting into tears at how thin he had become. Thereafter his decapitated head was exhibited at Nagasaki, after which it is uncertain what happened.

In Meiji times, an inscribed stone was discovered claiming to mark Shiro's resting place and was relocated to the castle (though it's thought now to be fake). It stands close to the grave of a leading attacker, so that the two men, mortal enemies in life, are symbolically joined in death. As I reflected on the irony, a three-year-old girl came up beside me and gingerly laid a sweet before the graves. "Gaikotsu ni okashi agetara mamotte kureru," she told me. "If you offer a sweet to the skeleton, its spirit will protect you." Her words spoke not only to the innocence of childhood, but to the deep-seated attachment to ancestor worship that characterizes Japanese religiosity.

Last thoughts

There was an excavation in progress at one side of the castle, and I wandered over to take a look. On the way I passed a collection of Jizo statues whose heads had been knocked off by the Christian defenders, and I tried not to dwell on the irony of the rebels themselves losing their heads following their defeat. Shogunate troops had made sure to demolish the castle walls, and boulders still lie strewn around today. From the ramparts I looked down on a lone motorcyclist clad in black leather, who was puffing contemplatively on a cigarette while gazing up at the castle. It was still early in the morning, but the site evidently held a strong fascination for him. It was after all the last major engagement of the Edo era, following which the country had been held tight in the straightjacket of Tokugawa isolation until the 1860s. The rebels who gathered here must have known they would come to a bloody end, but given the misery of their lives they had decided to make a stand. Had the archaeologists found anything interesting? I asked the man in charge.

"You mean, apart from bones," he said with a grin. "Just about everywhere you dig there are bones here, like a carpet. You're probably standing on some right now." He took me over to a small covering to see some of the finds they had uncovered. Along with skulls and pieces of bone were some small metal crosses. "You see these? They are made of lead from the bullets of the attackers. There were smiths in the castle, you see, and they took the lead bullets and bashed them into these small crosses. Sometimes we find them near the skull, even sometimes inside the jaw. Maybe the Christians swallowed them when they died. They knew the attackers would strip everything off the bodies, you see. They wanted to take the cross with them when they died to ease the way into heaven."

Perhaps the defenders had been simply kissing the crosses, I suggested, then noticing a line of festive lanterns strung across some nearby trees I asked what they were for. "Ah, those," said the archaeologist. "Those were for the cherry blossom festival." I'd read earlier of an annual parade in the town nearby, Minami Arima, when a boy representing Amakusa Shiro engages in mock combat with the shogunate general. Presumably the festivities were part of the wider celebration. Still, with all the bones around it seemed an odd venue for party making. After all the signboard at the top had proclaimed in no uncertain terms that YOU CAN FEEL THE SADNESS OF HISTORY HERE, EVEN AFTER 350 YEARS.

"Maybe we Japanese have a strange way of thinking," the archaeologist said. "We think it's good to share with the dead our happiness. The spirits of the dead will be happy to hear the sound of laughter, drinking and friendship. It will console them to know their descendants are happy. Maybe it's difficult for you to understand. . . ."

In the aftermath of the rebellion, the Tokugawa shogunate moved to clamp down on the possibility of any further disruptions. They punished the region's rulers for mismanagement, while taking the opportunity to drive the remaining Portuguese out of the country. For good measure, they even ordered children of mixed parentage to leave, as if the foreign blood might have been contaminated with the Christian virus. When the merchants of Macao sent a delegation in 1640 to ask for the resumption of trade, the Tokugawa showed they were in deadly earnest by executing sixty-one of the envoys while sparing thirteen to report back. In their message of explanation they linked the "worm-like barbarians of Macao" with the Shimabara rebels:

> If we had not destroyed and annihilated them as quickly
> as possible, their numbers would have increased, and

the revolt would have spread like the rebellion of Zhang Lu [in China in 184 CE]. . . . The instigators of this revolt were deserving of the severest punishment, and therefore a government envoy was sent to Nagasaki, warning your people that they should never return to this country, and if they did, everyone on board the ships would be killed.

It was convenient for the Tokugawa to link the rebels with the Macao meddlers, but can Shimabara be properly called a Catholic uprising? You certainly get that impression from visiting Hara Castle, for a large white cross dominates the ruined castle grounds. It suited the shogunate to portray it that way, because it gave them the pretext to put in place the final pieces of isolationism. It was helpful too for local daimyo, who sought to deflect blame for their misrule onto subversive Christians. Church historians were also eager to stress the strength of faith and to win sympathy for the victims. Modern commentators, however, prefer to see the uprising as a desperate outburst by starving peasants, which happened to develop a religious flavor due to the heady atmosphere. And what a heady atmosphere it was!

Many of the peasants were lapsed Catholics, whose imagination was seized by rumors circling their ranks. The Last Judgment was at hand; the famine was an apocalyptic punishment from God for renouncing his faith; it was the beginning of the end of the world. A prophecy by Father Marco Ferraro, who had worked in the area before being expelled, was particularly influential: "After 25 years a child of God will appear and save the people." It surely referred to the miraculously gifted Amakusa Shiro, who could speak Portuguese (he had studied in Nagasaki). He was said to be an angel who had come to lead the sixty-six provinces of Japan to Christianity, and rumor had it he could even walk on water. One popular story told how a bird had deposited an egg in his palm, which he broke open to reveal a painting of Jesus and a scroll of the Bible. Fired by such stories, the peasants fell in behind the religious agenda of the leadership and rallied to a Christian flag.

But who exactly was this Amakusa Shiro? How on earth could a scholarly sixteen-year-old (fifteen in some reports) become leader of a desperate uprising of peasants? It's curious that so much is known about the revolt, yet so little seems to be known about the youth who led it. We know for example exactly how many cannonballs the Dutch fired and from where (124 from the ship, and another 298 from an onshore position). Yet Amakusa Shiro remains an elusive figure, portrayed on the one hand as an effeminate youth in the *bishonen* (beautiful boy) tradition, and on the other as a restless and angry spirit. Perhaps, I reasoned, I would learn more about the real person in the Amakusa Islands, from which he derived his name. Japan has 6,852 islands in all, of which around 400 are inhabited: here was an opportunity to explore some with a reputation for peace and beauty. The quest for Hidden Christians was taking me to some providential places.

Chapter Eight

Post-Apocalypse
(Amakusa Islands)

Local hero

It's a short ferry ride to the Amakusa Islands from the port of Kuchinotsu on the Shimabara Peninsula. If it wasn't for the ferry, you'd hardly notice the port town, yet it played a key role in the early encounters of East and West, as Portuguese ships moored here. It was here too that Alessandro Valignano first landed in Japan, on his visit in 1570. There's a giant caricature of a Southern Barbarian opposite the ferry port: big, tall-nosed and ungainly, it exemplifies the mix of awe and bemusement that Japanese must have felt towards Westerners. The exotic clothing with its clashing colors and blooming pantaloons accentuates the strangeness. I posed next to the statue for a photo, seeing in the caricature one of my predecessors, but in a small maritime museum nearby I learned that I wasn't a Southern Barbarian at all. I was a *komoujin* (red-haired person), which is how the Dutch and English were dubbed to distinguish them from the Iberians. Being a redhead myself, I could hardly take exception.

On the other side of the strait, at the ominous Oniike (Devil's Pond), a statue of Shiro welcomes visitors to the Amakusa Islands. It's indicative of his status as local hero, and the islands boast an Amakusa Shiro Memorial Hall, to which I headed with eager anticipation. It turned out to be a disappointment, designed primarily to deprive day-trippers of their money. It started out grandly enough with a room given over to the Renaissance, not so much, one felt, out of historical background but a desire to display cheap reproductions of Raphael and Michelangelo. In the next section, Oda Nobunaga stood in solidarity with Francis Xavier, a curious combination given that they never met. "These two men helped sway the torch of Christianity in Japan," says the explanation unhelpfully. On the third floor, inexplicably, was a large meditation room with New Age music and uncomfortable beanbag chairs. But the biggest surprise was reserved for the end, where a statement proclaimed in large letters, "The Shimabara Uprising was the first time Japanese fought for equality and freedom," before expansively including it in a roll call of honor alongside the French Revolution and the American Civil War. Visionary stuff, indeed.

For all the high-tech 3D displays there was virtually nothing about the leader of the uprising. Given the name of the exhibition, this was puzzling, to say the least: "Yes, a lot of people say that," said the receptionist with a smile. Since she could offer little more, and since there was no expert on hand, I headed for the island capital of Hondo, where I'd arranged for a personal tour by Mr. Sato of the Association of Guides. Within minutes, I'd learned more than I had at the Memorial Hall. There were three different theories about Shiro's birthplace, for instance, but the probability was that his father was a vassal of Konishi Yukinaga, the Christian daimyo whose domain embraced the islands. When he died at the Battle of Sekigahara, many of his followers had become ronin (masterless samurai). Such was probably the case with Shiro's father.

The young rebel leader's real name had been Masuda Shiro Tokisada. According to local lore, he came to prominence through preaching of equality and dignity on the island of Oyano. "Why do we have to be treated like horses and cows?" he asked the congregation. "We do not ask for rice or even our life, but we insist on being treated as equal human beings." It was a revolutionary message for the downtrodden peasants, unused to being accorded respect or dignity. Word quickly spread of the boy wonder, and islanders flocked to listen to him.

That Shiro had studied in Nagasaki with the Jesuits would explain a lot about his rhetorical gifts, but one question still bothered me. Was he truly a leader, or had he simply been a figurehead chosen by a clique of samurai? Perhaps he'd even been duped into leadership? "We don't think like that," Sato-san said, as if speaking for the islands as a whole. "We think he was a leader, because people wanted to follow him, even if it meant death. They knew they couldn't win, but they believed in him. He was an orator, you see. He could make people believe in what he said."

Items related to the Shimabara Uprising have been brought together at Shirayama Park, which is where Mr. Sato was taking me, and on the way we passed houses with outsize New Year decorations strung above their doorway. The thickly pleated rice rope bore a colorful assortment of decorations: ferns, oranges, fans, arrows, even plastic lobsters. Yet this was May: why on earth were New Year decorations still up? "It's a special custom here," explained Sato-san. "It started in the Edo period after the Uprising as a way to show that the household was not Christian. New Year is a Shinto festival, and Christians were not supposed to celebrate that. So people put up large decorations to prove they were not Christian and left them up all year. Still we do like that now," he added.

At the Memorial Park was a large burial mound for the remains of those who died in the uprising, whether rebel or attacker. Every month a joint requiem service by Catholics and Buddhists is held. Nearby is a collection of Hidden Christian gravestones, which were identified in modern times and gathered here in the park. Most bear a cross, though on some it is cunningly disguised to look like the Japanese numeral for ten or a thousand. There was a memorial too for a young girl named Michika, to whom Shiro had supposedly given a *temari* (woven ball) as a parting gift. The ball is Chinese in origin, made by carefully wrapping pieces of silk fabric around a central core, and Sato-san suggested it was a special gift because it would have been brought by the Portuguese from Macao. Legend has it the couple were in love and that when she heard of his death, she shut herself away and made *temari* over and over again.

The focal point of the park is the Kirishitan Kan (Christian Hall), where the star exhibit is the battle flag around which the Shimabara rebels rallied. The bloodstained and battle-scarred original is only exhibited on special occasions, but a replica is on permanent show and it's a curious item. Battle pennants of the age are familiar from films like Kurosawa's *Ran* (1985), in which samurai wear symbols of the lord they serve, but here was a completely different kind of image. It shows a chalice and host being worshipped by angels, beneath which runs a slogan in Portuguese: "Worship the Most Holy Sacrament." What could starving peasants have made of that? No doubt the very foreignness of the words gave them a magical allure, but what of the imagery: did they link the body and blood of Christ with their own imminent demise? Was this as close as the Japanese got to fighting for the Holy Grail?

The flag is strikingly Western and surprisingly colorful: the chalice is yellow, the angel's wings green and reddish-brown. It was the work of Yamada Emosaku, presumed to have picked up his skills in Nagasaki, where a Jesuit priest was training native artists. Some of these Japanese were so gifted that by 1601 Father Guerreiro was able to report that "nowadays the churches in Japan are decorated with such rich and excellent altarpieces that one can compare them with those made in Europe." It's thought that Emosaku worked for the Shimabara daimyo in his early career, doing oil paintings; later he participated in the uprising and became the sole survivor. Sole survivor?! How on earth could you become the sole survivor of 37,000 slaughtered people? By turning traitor is the supposition, and by supplying information to your former employer about the defensive positions. Later reports tell of Emosaku working in Edo, where he apparently flourished. Looking at his flag, I thought not so much of the uprising but of the great gulf between the artist and his art. It's part of the fascination of life that inspiration so often dwells in the most flawed of characters: even the most villainous traitor is capable of rare beauty.

Island tour

From Shirayama Park, Sato-san drove me around the island to see what had happened in the years following the rebellion, when the shogunate took direct control of the area. Our first stop was the reconstructed Tomioka Castle, where a large statue portrays the man appointed governor in the wake of the uprising, Suzuki Shigenari (1588–1653). Together with his elder brother Shosan, a Zen Buddhist monk who wrote a strong condemnation of Christianity (*Ha Kirishitan*), he redirected the religious sympathies of the islanders by building new temples and shrines. Whole villages had joined in the Shimabara Uprising and been wiped out as a result: to replace them the governor promoted immigration and asked the shogunate to cut the tax base by half. When the request was refused, he committed seppuku. It made him a local hero, and to this day the islanders honor his memory (some shrines are dedicated to him). A pamphlet by the local council describes him "with profound esteem" as having helped revitalize the broken community. "We are very grateful to him," Sato-san said.

As elsewhere, the islanders had to register with Buddhist temples and to trample on the *fumie* every year. Surveillance was strict, and there were generous rewards for informants. Yet pockets of Hidden Christians held out—particularly in the villages of Oe and Sakitsu. The road along which we were headed, named the Sunset Line, leads into the Japan of the past, where wooden houses huddle against forested hillsides and old people scrape seaweed off rocks. The clayish soil is not fertile enough for rice, but it does sustain crops of beans, lettuce, potato and citrus fruit. In the few flat areas of habitation, cultivation had eradicated all the trees, such that the forest line along the foot of the hills made for a clear divide between the human world and the wild. Graves were set at the base of the hills, rising up the lower slopes, and in the Japanese imagination the unseen world beyond was a fearful realm of strange creatures and ghostly spirits. It was such settings as this that formed the spiritual landscape of the nation.

After passing through a village called, intriguingly, Devil's Inlet, we came to a small shrine that stood forlorn like a dilapidated hut. Next to it was a dried-up waterfall, and even the bottle of saké placed as an offering to the *kami* stood empty. It was a sorry sight that spoke of the neglect and depopulation that plagues remote areas of rural Japan these days. The loss of young folk and an aging population make it difficult to maintain the traditions of the past. In Shinto belief, the *kami* need constant attention: ignore them and they will wither or move away. In other words, if you fail to tend the environment, you destroy the spirit of place. So much of Shinto makes sense in this way that I couldn't help wondering why the locals would have turned to a foreign faith that denounced the native religion as evil.

It's said that one of the reasons Christianity was able to take hold in the islands was that most of the population belonged to the closest Buddhist equivalent, the Jodo Shinshu sect (True Pure Land Faith). In the figure of Amida, the sect has a deity who offers salvation in the next life if one has faith. His attendant, Kannon, acts as an intermediary between the divine world and that of humans. In a sense, the groundwork for the reception of Christianity had already been done, and the missionaries were plowing fertile soil. What did Sato think?

"Equality," he said. "Equality and dignity. Poor people here weren't used to that. They were used to being underlings, the lowest of the low. So they really liked the idea of everyone being equal. And of the poor being rich after death and living a good life, while the powerful would not. I think they wanted to believe that very much. So they believed very strongly. Even punishment or death would not change them. And they could support each other as brothers. They had a kind of strength because of that."

"So how about the islanders now?" I asked. "Are they interested in the Christian past?"

"No," he said with a laugh. "Not really. Just they care about the present, about their daily life. They don't like trouble."

"Trouble?"

"Yes. The Christians caused trouble, they think. Otherwise they wouldn't have been punished and treated as criminals."

Hidden secrets

The village of Oe boasts a striking white-walled church, built in 1933 and set on a small hill that dominates the surrounding countryside. Below it stands the Rosario Museum, which focuses on the life of Hidden Christians. They were able to organize themselves, the exhibition explains, because even before the missionaries were hounded out of existence, self-help organizations were in place that helped compensate for the high ratio of believers to priests. The Works of Mercy Confraternities were set up by Luis Almeida to serve the sick and needy, and the Santa Maria Confraternity organized prayer meetings. In addition to the Jesuits, other Catholic orders had organized groups, such as the Dominican-led Confraternity of the Rosary. A prominent role had been played by the Confraternity of the Blessed Sacrament, dedicated to preparing believers for the Eucharist. Its members had played a key role at Shimabara, which may explain why the flag portrayed the host and chalice. Like a mantra, followers repeated even to their very last breath, "May Jesus of the Blessed Sacrament be praised."

Even before the era of persecution, the paucity of priests meant lay groups performed many of the church's functions. It meant too that the teachings behind them were not always fully absorbed, but transmitted in half-understood manner. As a result, when the Hidden Christian groups were formed, they were often dependent on shaky information, for there were no priests or Bibles to tell them otherwise. The groups divided important functions between members: one person took charge of the records and organized gatherings (*chokata*); one was in charge of baptisms (*mizukata*); another acted as catechist (*oshiekata*). Worship centered around prayers known as *orashio* (from *oratio*), which were memorized and handed down orally from generation to generation.

To disguise their practice, the Hidden Christians used some ingenious tricks, and a whole room of the museum is given over to locally made clay dolls showing a *yamamba* (mountain hag), which substituted for the Virgin Mary. Another exhibit displays a secret message encoded in pictographs, for it shows a mountain (*san* in Japanese); a rice field (*ta*); a circle (*maru*); and a roof (*ya*)—the images therefore read: *Santa Maruya* (i.e. Santa Maria: *maru* in Japanese gives a sense of roundness, appropriate for a pregnant woman). There's also a gravestone whose Buddhist slogan, "Namu Amida Butsu," is arranged in the form of a cross. Even more intriguing is a magic pot used to "catch" sutras. All citizens were obliged by law to hold Buddhist funerals, and since

Hidden Christians believed this would compromise the chance of entering heaven, they were anxious to counteract the effect. Accordingly, they filled the pot with holy water, and during the ceremony someone would sit in a neighboring room to recite *orashio* while dipping a rosary in and out of the water. In this way it was thought the sutra would enter the pot and be nullified.

In the early years, the Amakusa Christians held services in caves or the middle of woods, where a simple mound of earth, easily destroyed in case of emergency, served as an altar. With their *yamamba* clay dolls, the outdoor gatherings must have resembled those of witches that were causing so much alarm in Europe at the time. Provision for worship was also made in secret parts of private houses, and the museum contains a model of an actual room uncovered in Meiji times. It's a simple attic, the ladder to which was concealed behind a sliding wall panel. Beneath the eaves there was space for three or four believers to kneel in prayer. Here a family had performed the rituals they believed would bring them salvation.

And so, amazingly, the Hidden Christians continued for two hundred years, handing down prayers, passing on treasured items, living a double life—Buddhist in name, Kirishitan in belief. With the passage of time, complacency must have set in, for in 1805 a ritual was held at a temple after which participants left behind evidence of having eaten beef. It was something Buddhists would not do, and an informer alerted the authorities. The subsequent investigation unearthed a massive 5,205 Christians—about half the area's population. It presented a dilemma for those in power, for should the Hidden Christians all be exiled or executed it would decimate the tax base. A solution was found by declaring that the group was engaged in "misguided conduct of religion" as if unaware of what they were doing—a rare example of Christians escaping punishment in 250 years of persecution.

Following our visit to the museum, Sato-san and I wandered up the hill to the Oe Church. Above the altar was a painting of Saint Gabriel visiting Mary, both very European in appearance, while to the left was a statue of a Japanese man in a kimono and *chomage* hairstyle holding out a hand to a young boy. It was Paul Miki, together with the twelve-year-old crucified with him at Nagasaki. We fell into conversation with a nun who happened to be there, and I took the opportunity to ask about the number of Catholics in the area. "We are losing members," she said. "Because they are old. Like me," she said with a laugh. "Here and in Sakitsu we had eight hundred members when the church was built. But now we have only five hundred members. And young people are moving away. They don't want to live here, you see."

When she learned we were going to Sakitsu, she told us to be sure to visit the Santa Maria statue at the harbor for the protection of fishermen. "They all cross themselves when passing the statue on their way to go fishing," she said, "even the Buddhists." Though it features on tourist brochures, Sato-san had never seen it close up and had trouble tracking it down. Like the famous Copenhagen mermaid, it is hard to locate and less imposing in reality than in photographs—a case of distance lending enchantment. The Gothic-style church, on the other hand, with its waterside location, was a most handsome feature, and from the opposite side of the bay it gave the village the air of southern Europe. It was selected improbably as one of the "100 Best Scenes with a Japanese Flavor," under the dubious title: "Christian village of Sakitsu." Nonetheless, it's suggestive of how things might have turned out had the Catholic mission succeeded. As with the grandiose churches the Spanish built in the Philippines, the religion would surely have taken root and grown into the local landscape.

Inside the church, chairs were set out on top of tatami in an uneasy compromise of East and West. I mentioned it to an elderly man with bent back and wrinkled features taking a rest after tending the garden. "Ha ha," he responded with a twinkle in his eye. "It's because the other members are so old. They can't even sit on tatami. I'm one of the youngest. I'm still *genki*. That's why I have to do the gardening," he said with a toothless grin.

From the church, a path led to the top of the nearby hill, where an electronic church bell has been installed to ring out over the village. Halfway up was a small Konpira Shrine dedicated to the *kami* of sailors, where an elderly woman was busy with brush and broom in the diligent manner of the Japanese. She had the cheerful healthiness of someone who has lived all her life close to the elements, and I asked if people from the church stopped off sometimes on their way to the bell. "Oh yes, some do," she said. "They say a prayer to protect them. *Kami*, God, same same," she said with a laugh. "They all protect us if we pray." Islanders may have narrow horizons in one sense, but in another their vision is unfettered.

The last port of call on our island tour was the former site of Amakusa Collegio, set up in 1591. The Jesuits had moved their seminary to the island because the remoteness offered greater security at a time of instability. Now a small museum stands on the site, featuring European musical instruments such as lute and harpsichord. It's a reminder of the emphasis the Jesuits placed on the charm of music as a means of conversion. There's also a full-scale replica of the printing press brought by Alessandro Valiginano on his return with the Four Envoys in 1590. For over seven years it had been in production here, during which time some thirty different books were issued. As well as dictionaries and doctrinal treatises, there were cultural works such as *Aesop's Fables*.

The most influential work produced by the Amakusa press was *Dochirina Kirishitan* (1591), an explanation of Christian teaching translated from a Portuguese catechism. Interestingly, it starts with the European format of a teacher testing a pupil, but then reverses it to suit Japanese tastes, with a disciple asking a *sensei* (teacher) for answers. "Jesus Cristo was as tall as ordinary people in the world; how is he able to exist entirely in the small *hostia*?" is one such example. Among the modifications of the original was an explanation of Christ's self-sacrifice in terms of *giri* (obligation); emphasis on the power of the cross to deal with restless spirits; and, remarkably, an amendment to the fifth commandment to allow killing should a lord have good reason to punish a vassal.

For security reasons, the press was moved to Nagasaki in 1597, where it continued putting out works until 1612. By that time it had issued approximately a hundred books in all, some in kanji, some in *romaji*, and some in European languages. They were intended for Japanese studying theology as well as Europeans studying Japanese. The print run of 1,500 was surprisingly large, compared with the norm of 300 to 500 copies produced by European presses. "Historians say that the Collegio was the largest publisher in the world at that time," boasts the museum pamphlet. Imagine that! This charming backwater was once churning out books on a scale not seen anywhere else on earth.

Double crosser

One of the people associated with the press was the intriguing Fukansai Fabian (aka Fabian Fukan (c.1565–1621). Once a prominent Christian, he became a prominent anti-Christian. He thus has the distinction of being not only the first Japanese to write a full defense of Christianity, but the first to write a full refutation too. Intellectually gifted, he was able to argue both sides of the debate, either with scholastic logic or oriental reasoning. Though his early life is unclear, it seems he studied at a Zen monastery in Kyoto before joining the Jesuits in his late teen.

The training in Latin and theology led him into the academic side of the order, and in 1595 he published an abridged and romanized version of the *Heike Monogatari* with the Amakusa press. It has been championed as the first ever work of *nihonjin-ron* (the debate about what it means to be Japanese) because of the way it illustrates the complex ties of social obligation that are supposedly difficult for foreigners to understand.

In *Myotei Mundo* (1605), Fabian wrote a work of Christian apologetics that is of interest as being the first of its kind by a Japanese. It consists of a dialogue between two Christian nuns, one a novice and the other her instructor. The book proposes the superiority of a God of Creation to Japanese deities. Buddhist gods are dismissed as dead humans, while the Shinto creation myth is portrayed as a lewd sexual act in which Japan is the product—quite literally—of divine emission. By contrast, Christianity with its message of spiritual brotherhood is seen as offering not only the possibility of peace in this world but the chance of salvation in a future life.

Not long after writing the book, Fabian left the Jesuits for reasons that are unclear. There were reports of his having run away with a nun: he would not have been the first! In a later book he complained of not being promoted to the priesthood, so it may be that his decision to leave the Jesuits stemmed from frustration in more than one sense. Thereafter he apparently worked for the anti-Christian campaign in Nagasaki, and the next mention of him is as the author of *Hadaisu* (1620) (literally, "Against God," though translated by George Elison as *Deus Destroyed*). Here he mocked Christianity and openly scorned the idea of a Creator. Anyone who wanted to create a universe must be a supreme egoist, he argued. Besides, if God was almighty, how come he didn't help Christians who were being tortured and executed? If he was omniscient, how come he didn't foresee the fall of the angels? And if he was all-merciful, why did he create eternal hell? As for those who worshipped him, they were clearly a threat to the security of the nation:

> The first commandment urges disobedience to the orders of the sovereign or father if compliance would mean denial of Deus's will; it entreats one to hold life itself cheap in such a situation. In this respect lurks the intention to subvert and usurp the country, to extinguish Buddha's Law and Royal Sway. Quick, quick! Put this gang in stocks and shackles! . . . The spread of such a cursed doctrine is completely the working of the devil.

The portrayal reflected the changing times, for whereas *Myotei Mondo* had come out at a time when Christianity was tolerated, *Hadaiusu* belonged to an age in which the religion was a state enemy. Fabian's skills as a polemicist paved the way for a whole genre of anti-Christian literature: he even appeared as a character himself in *Kirishitan Monogatari* (*The Christian Story*), where he is cast as a sorcerer, and in *Nanbanji Kohaiki* (*Rise and Fall of the Temple of the Southern Barbarians*) in which he is a cunning indoctrinator. The latter, published around 1639, gave a satirical overview of Christianity in Japan, portraying the faith as a weird kind of Buddhism in which people sit in circles, confess their sins and flog themselves until they bleed. In dispute with a Buddhist priest, the fictional Fabian is left speechless by probing questions about why a crucified criminal should be a focus for worship. Like a beaten dog, he runs off yelping in pain.

I'd become immersed in a world of books in contemplation of the Amakusa press, and stepping out of the museum I drew some deep lungfuls of the wholesome sea air and looked along the coastline. How strange to think that at one time black-robed priests had wandered here among the simple fisherfolk, deep in

their studies of Latin or Church theology. In this timeless landscape, unspoiled and unassuming, had once existed the cutting
edge of East and West. Few have better expressed that interaction
than the Catholic novelist Endo Shusaku, whose works explore
the clash of European thinking with that of the Japanese. His
most famous book, *Silence*, is set in the years that follow the
Shimabara Uprising and the events take place in an area just
north of Nagasaki called Sotome. It was there that my thoughts
now turned.

Chapter Nine

Silence
(Sotome)

Camouflage

Karematsu Jinja in Sotome is a curious affair: it's a Shinto-style shrine for a Christian martyr named San Jiwan-sama. Not much is known about him, though he's presumed to have been a Portuguese priest named Juan who was active in the area in the age of persecution. He's said to have hidden on the Karematsu hill, where a woman called Oen brought him food every day. One winter she was prevented by snow, and he died of cold and hunger. To the Hidden Christians of the area, he was a revered figure, who was given the posthumous title of *san* (from the Portuguese for "saint").

Nowadays, Sotome is technically a part of Nagasaki City, though puzzlingly it lies forty minutes away along a pleasant road that takes one deep into the countryside. In the past the only way to reach the isolated villages was by sea, and the priest would have stolen ashore by boat as he went about ministering to the coastal communities. The area had first been Christianized in the 1560s when it was part of the domain of Omura Sumitada. By 1614, when Christianity was banned, a whole generation had been raised from birth as Catholic, but with the onset of persecution roughly half the population apostatized and the rest became Hidden Christians. It was in their service that San Jiwan ministered, at risk to his life. Legend has him mysteriously coming and going—a reference no doubt to his furtive appearances under cover of darkness.

The priest's burial place was marked by two large pine trees (*karematsu* means "withered pines"). It became a focus of worship for the area's believers, and fishermen out at sea would pray as they passed by. Worshippers gathered on the hill at the base of an enormous boulder that faces the grave, known as the Prayer Rock. It reminded me of the sacred rocks (*iwakura*) of Shinto: perhaps the villagers were closer to pagan roots than they realized. In ancient Japan it was thought that spirits could descend into objects, and rocks served as an obvious symbol of immortality. Similarly for the Hidden Christians, there was a sense of San Jiwan having entered into the pines that marked his grave, and the trees were accordingly treated as sacred—much like the *shinboku* (divine trees) of Shinto shrines, indeed.

To avoid suspicion, veneration of San Jiwan was camouflaged as worship of a *kami*. It made good sense, since the hill is of the wooded type often celebrated in Shinto. Even in modern times, when the need for subterfuge had long passed, the honoring of San Jiwan continues in Shinto style as if entirely natural. Until the 1930s there was a small shrine (*hokora*), where soldiers going off to war would pay respects, then in the late 1930s a building was erected (which was reconstructed in 2002). It is a rare instance of a Shinto-style shrine with no torii. Inside are pieces of the original pine trees, and a grave with an inscription to San Jiwan, PAPPA CONFESORU—a faux Latin tribute to the priest-confessor.

Bastian's hut

San Jiwan had a Japanese aide named Bastian (short for Sebastian), who is remembered for a calendar he compiled to calculate the cycle of Christian festivals. It was no easy matter, for the lunar-based calendar used in Japan was at complete odds with European dates (only after the Meiji Restoration of 1868 was the Western calendar adopted). Until 1618 the Jesuits printed their own calendars, following which they had to be smuggled in from Macao. The last to arrive was that for 1634. Thereafter Bastian's calendar became a treasured item, enabling underground Christians to convert solar festivals to lunar as well as to calculate movable rites such as Easter. There are copies in a Sotome museum, and I was surprised by the simplicity—a few small sheets of handwritten paper, marked into weeks with notes for special days.

In his youth, Bastian had been gatekeeper at a Buddhist temple, but after converting he became a Jesuit *dojuku* (lay helper). The duties of the *dojuku* consisted mainly in assisting priests, but they were also able to preach and give instruction. In 1604 there were more than 150 of them, and after the Church went underground they played a vital role in serving priestless communities. Bastian is a case in point: for over twenty years he worked clandestinely to pass on the faith and almost single-handedly helped sustain the groups of isolated Christians.

Among the myths about Bastian, the most important concerns the origins of his calendar. The story goes that he and Jiwan had arrived secretly on the Sotome coast, when the priest suddenly announced that he had to return home and walked off across the surface of the sea. Dismayed, Bastian fasted for twenty-one days and prayed for his mentor's return: he was rewarded with a vision in which San Jiwan vouchsafed the calendrical cycle. It was of vital importance, for it provided believers with the schedule of rituals that facilitated eternal salvation.

Handed down in miraculous fashion, the calendar became imbued with semi-divine status and the person in charge—the *chokata* (keeper of the notes)—acted as leader of the Hidden Christian groups. It's been suggested the primacy derived from the importance of religious calendars in the Japanese tradition, to which Daoism had added the notion of "lucky" and "unlucky" days. Similarly, the Hidden Christians observed special days when working was not supposed to be done, and their attachment to the calendar is reflected in modern-day descendants who refer to themselves not as Hidden Christians but as *motocho* (people of the original calendar) or *furucho* (old calendar).

About five miles north of Karematsu Shrine stands the hut where Bastian lived while in hiding. The path to it takes one away from the trappings of civilization into a world of bamboo and pine, where an isolated hut stands on the valley floor. Nearby is a fresh flowing stream from which water was drawn for baptism. There was once a wooden hut with a thatched roof, but it was destroyed by a storm in 1993 and replaced with a more solid building. It remains even now an idyllic setting, reminiscent of the idealized picture of the hermit's life in Kamo no Chomei's *Hojoki* (1212). But whereas the Buddhist recluse sought solace in solitude, Bastian went out in the service of others. When victims of the Kohri persecution of 1657 were thrown into the sea, their arms wrapped in straw jackets to prevent swimming, he recovered the bodies and gave them a Christian funeral.

In the same year, the outlaw Christian was given away by smoke from his cooking fire (another version has him betrayed by a Judas-like figure). For over two years he was held and tortured, then decapitated, but before his death he made four prophecies: that his executioners would be protected for seven generations, after which it would be difficult to save them; that priests would come in black boats and hear confessions every week; that there would be an age when Christians were free to walk and sing hymns in a loud voice; and that non-Christians would give way to them in the street. Taken as a whole, the implication was that foreign missionaries would return after seven generations and inaugurate a time of toleration—which is exactly what happened. The Black Ships of Commodore Perry arrived from the United States in 1853, and de facto legalization of Christianity followed twenty years later. It came 214 years after Bastian's death, which if one calculates a generation at thirty years was indeed seven generations. More than a martyr, it made the Sotome man a prophet of biblical proportions.

Fact and fiction

When the novelist Endo Shusaku (1923–96) came to Sotome, he saw in the rugged shoreline and isolated villages, just the location he sought for a story formulating in his mind. It was to become his most celebrated novel, *Silence* (1965), and was set in the years following the Shimabara Uprising, around the time of San Jiwan and Bastian, when Christians were a hunted species. He had first hit on the idea during a visit to Nagasaki, when his imagination was seized by the dark stains on a *fumie* caused by thousands of feet treading on the brass icon. Many of their owners had returned home to practice their faith in secret. What kind of people were they, and how did they feel about the act of betrayal? What would he himself have done? All too aware of his own weakness, the author knew that he too would have been a Hidden Christian.

During his research, Endo came across the curious case of Christovao Ferreira (1580–1650). The Portuguese priest had arrived in the country as a twenty-nine-year-old and gone underground after the 1614 ban, living rough and moving around at night. His dedication led eventually to appointment as Vice Provincial, head of the Japanese Jesuits in Japan. Not long afterwards, in 1634, he was arrested. Together with seven others he was suspended upside down over ordure in the most feared of Japanese tortures—the pit. After six hours he gave the signal that he was ready to recant, though none of the others did. One survived for an astonishing nine days.

For the inquisitor Inoue Chikugo (c.1584–1661), Ferreira's apostasy was a prize achievement. As a former Christian himself, he sought to subvert the Church's policy of martyrdom by breaking prisoners physically and psychologically. Torture methods designed to produce extremes of pain were alternated with debate, persuasion and temptation. Particular attention was given to "turning" foreign priests. The goal was a signed confession, following which the apostate would be given a Japanese name and made to live with a wife (often the widow of a criminal). Such was the case with Ferreira, who took the name of Suwano Chuan.

Reports followed of Ferreira assisting at the interrogation of foreigners, and in 1637 three years after the apostasy, an anti-Christian tract appeared called *A Disclosure of Falsehoods*. It was signed by "Chief Bateren of Japan and Macao, Christovao Ferreira, reformed in religion and turned an adherent of Zen." It contained some stinging criticisms of his former faith. God could not possibly be all-powerful, because he failed to help those being persecuted. And why didn't he make Adam, Eve and the rest of humankind sinless, given that the Virgin Mary was? As for God's followers, the Ten Commandments forbade stealing, but Europeans went to other countries and brazenly robbed the people of their land. Those Christians were bad news!

When report of the apostasy reached the West, it caused a sensation and there was disbelief that a senior representative could disgrace Catholicism in such manner. The whole rock-like foundation of the Church was shaken, leading to prayers and penance on Ferreira's behalf. Volunteers offered themselves for martyrdom in his stead, and from Macao the Visitator Antonio Rubino organized groups to enter Japan and persuade the former

Vice Provincial to withdraw his recantation. It amounted to a suicide mission, for the consequences of violating Japan's isolation policy were well known.

The first group, including Rubino himself, arrived in southern Kyushu in 1642 but was quickly captured. After seven months of interrogation, they were subjected to the pit and died. The second group, led by Giuseppe Chiara, arrived the next year in northern Kyushu but fared no better. This time, however, the whole group of ten apostatized—a shock given that the men were volunteers. Ferreira had assisted at the interrogation of both groups, and it was this that intrigued Endo Shusaku. What was going on in the minds of the Europeans, and what kind of conversation passed between them?

In his novel, Endo welded fact to fiction by having Christovao Ferreira interact with an imaginary priest called Sebastian Rodrigues. The latter was Portuguese, whereas his real-life model (Giuseppe Chiara) had been Italian. The narrative charts the course of Rodriques after arriving in Japan with a fellow missionary called Francisco Garrpe. His hope is to be of service to isolated Christians, while at the same time establishing the truth about his former teacher, Ferreira. He seems destined for martyrdom—it is what he has been trained for; it is what he believes in; it is what he has volunteered for. Yet whereas Garrpe dies in the service of others, Rodrigues renounces his faith after being betrayed to the authorities by a lapsed Christian named Kichijiro. The apostate ends the book living as a Japanese, yet in his heart he continues to be a believer who is convinced that Jesus would have acted the same way. In this way the novel can be read as a tale of death and rebirth: a Portuguese priest who arrives in Japan with European convictions is reborn as a Hidden Christian called Okada San'emon.

East meets West

Sotome has taken Endo to its heart, and in 2000 the Endo Shusaku Literary Museum was built in celebration of *Silence*. It stands on a promontory with superb views of headland and open sea. Inside are manuscripts, personal items, writing desk and library. There are film posters too, one of which is for *Chinmoku* (1971), the Japanese title of *Silence*. The adaptation enjoyed reasonable success, and though personally I had misgivings about the English-speaking lead, the coastal scenes and realistic depictions of peasant life linger in the mind.

The museum affords the opportunity to reflect on Endo's writings, the great theme of which is the difficulty of applying a Western religion to a Japanese context. It was something with which he struggled all his life, after being baptised to please his mother at the age of twelve. Newly divorced, she had returned to Japan from Manchuria and in her distress turned for consolation to the faith of her sister. When she converted, her son joined her. "I was baptised against my will," Endo wrote in "Kirishitan and Today": "I did not choose Christianity as in choosing a lover, but I accepted it as in accepting a bride chosen by my parents. When I was a student, I often told this bride that we should be divorced, but she would not consent to it. So I had to go on with my married life."

He wrote later of the European religion feeling like "a badly-fitted suit" on his Japanese body, and for years he was plagued by doubt, confusion and a shallow faith. In wartime Japan he was bullied for having the religion of his enemies, and in postwar France, where he studied literature, he suffered from a deep sense of isolation. Tuberculosis and health complications resulted in two and a half years in the hospital, with three major operations and near-death experiences. It led to a newfound belief that was directed not to the triumphant and all-conquering Christ that he had encountered in Europe but to an outcast Jesus filled with compassion for the suffering of others.

The turning point of *Silence* comes when prosecutors confront Rodrigues with the *fumie*. Up to that point God has remained silent, despite the agonies suffered by his followers. Even the resolute Rodriques is moved to doubt in his existence. At the same time he knows that his obduracy is causing suffering to others, and his captors threaten to execute innocent villagers if he refuses to recant. It makes him realize his desire for martyrdom is egotistical, and that real self-sacrifice would be to give up his ambition. The decisive moment comes as he looks at the face of Jesus on the *fumie*, which seems to say to him, "Trample! trample! I more than anyone know of the pain in your foot. Trample! It was to be trampled on that I was born into this world."

Treading on the *fumie* is the first "step" in the transformation of the ego-driven European. It leads him to revise his earlier views: "Our Lord was not silent," he says at the end. "Even if he had been silent, my life until this day would have spoken of him." The understanding shows how much he has been changed by time in the country, for silence has always been part of the Japanese way. "We Japanese think we can better express our feelings by silence," Lafcadio Hearn was once told. I've been told much the same thing.

By the end of the book, a familiar pattern has emerged: a foreigner who came to change Japan ends up being changed himself. In the journey from priest to Hidden Christian, Rodrigues comes to espouse a Japanese type of Catholicism hung around a maternal Jesus. The idea was developed by Endo in *A Life of Jesus* (1973), in which he asserts that "the Japanese tend to seek in their gods and buddhas a warm-hearted mother rather than a stern father." His claim finds support in the primacy of the sun goddess Amaterasu in Shinto; the popularity of a feminized Kannon in Buddhism; and the ready adoption of the Virgin Mary by Hidden Christians. "Because I am Japanese—and because I entertain a strong sense of love towards my mother—this 'magna mater' archetype becomes active whenever I think of Christ," he wrote in an essay, "Novels I Have Loved." Caring, forgiving and ever-present—Endo's Son of God reflects the qualities of a Japanese mother.

For the psychologist Doi Takeo, the over-dependency of Japanese on their mothers leads to an inability to achieve full adulthood, and in his best-selling book *Anatomy of Dependence* (1971) he explored the consequences. It helps explain some of the most puzzling traits of the culture—the self-consciousness; the sensitivity to criticism; the reluctance to take responsibility; the cult of the cute; even the dependency on America. "Japan is a nation of twelve-year-olds," General MacArthur said in a much-maligned statement. Perhaps in his own crass way the general was getting at something similar to Doi. If Sigmund Freud was right about religious deities being parental figures writ large, then Doi's theory and the feminine orientation of Japanese religiosity may well be linked.

In shaping his ideas, Endo drew on Eric Fromm's distinction between a mother religion in which deities are nurturing and forgiving, and a father religion in which God is fearful, judgmental and punitive. The novelist also saw the Japanese as more oriented to life in this world than the next, and in *Silence* he has Ferreira say that "The Japanese are not able to think of God completely divorced from man . . . the Japanese cannot think of an existence that transcends the human." In addition, the polytheistic inclinations of the culture meant that for Endo the whole religious mindset was inimical to the European faith: "This country is a swamp . . . a more terrible swamp than you can imagine. Whenever you plant a sapling in this swamp the roots begin to rot; the leaves grow yellow and wither. And we have planted the sapling of Christianity in this swamp."

The ability to accept multiple truths is one of Japan's salient traits. It's written into the country's history: to the animism and ancestor worship of ancient times were added layers of Buddhism, Taoism and Confucianism. The result was a richly diverse syncretic mix, which reconciled apparently contradictory beliefs. It was totally at odds with the cold dualities of the Rationalist tradition: "Yes or no" is how Japanese see the forced choices of the West. Their own preference is for "Maybe," and the tendency to ambiguity and vagueness contrasts with the black-and-white certainties of the West. It leads to such cultural traits as the vogue for Christian weddings, even though participants have no interest in the religion. If all gods are equally valid, then it makes sense to choose a style of wedding that looks the prettiest. Form triumphs over function. It was a trait I was coming to recognize in Hidden Christians too.

Connecting

When Endo's novel came out in the 1960s, there was much praise for the force of the writing, and the book became a best-seller. Yet there were those who took exception, particularly among Catholics. An irreconcilable East and West was contrary to the idea of universalism, and the narrative sympathy with apostasy upset some. As a result, the book was put on the blacklist by at least two dioceses, and when Endo's name came up as a candidate for the Nobel Prize there were some Japanese Catholics who opposed it. Here in Sotome a memorial stone set up to honor the novel was defaced in protest in 1999. It bears a quotation from the book that seems tellingly apt: "Humanity is so sad, Lord, and the ocean so blue."

Endo's championing of a maternal Jesus also proved contentious, and fellow novelist Shiba Ryotaro commented: "Endo theology is Pure Land teaching. It is possible to replace his God with Amida." Buddhist deities had long been associated with feminine qualities, and the thirteenth-century founder of the True Pure Land sect, Shinran, wrote that "Like the mother protecting her child in her deep love, so do a thousand Nyorai remember the living in their deep love and compassion." It seemed then that Endo had dressed the foreign religion in native garb, and the author himself said as much: "I wrote in a postscript that Rodrigues's last words smacked of Protestantism, but to tell the truth I feel that in those words is to be found a kind of reconciliation of Catholicism and Pure Land Buddhism." Like his country, the author's instincts were syncretic.

One of those for whom the novel struck a chord was the American director, Martin Scorsese, who for long has harbored plans to make a film adaptation (already in the 1990s he asked Endo personally for permission). In 2009, he made a reconnaissance trip to Sotome and spent two or three hours at the museum engaged in research and discussion. He has spoken of the film as close to his heart and a pet project, different from his studio-produced movies. But what would draw a New York director famed for gangster movies to a tale of seventeenth-century Japan?

Raised a Catholic, Scorsese attended a seminary in his youth and nurtured thoughts of becoming a priest. He chose film instead: "I realized that the Catholic vocation was, in a sense, through the screen for me," he said. Like Endo he suffered doubt and a weak faith, commenting that "I'm a lapsed Catholic. But I am Roman Catholic—there's no way out of it." A clue to what drew him to *Silence* can be found in his film *The Last Temptation of Christ* (1988), starring Willem Dafoe. Based on a book by Nikos Kazantzakis, it explores Jesus as a human being rather than divine miracle worker: in place of a blue-eyed savior is a down-

and-out dirty figure. The unorthodox view proved controversial, and a dream sequence of marriage to Mary Magdalene caused outrage in some quarters. Feelings ran so high in the United States that there was protest, violence and property damage. In France, movie theaters were vandalized, and two were destroyed by fire. Scorsese's parish priest once remarked that the director's films had "too much Good Friday and not enough Easter Sunday." Scorsese responded by saying it was the tortured Jesus rather than the Messiah to whom he was drawn. Endo said much the same thing.

Yet the religious angle is not the only aspect that attracted the American to *Silence*. "It raises a lot of problems about foreign cultures coming and imposing their way of thinking on another culture they know nothing about," he told a reporter for the AP. In the wake of the Iraq fiasco, it prompts thoughts about the connections between Rome in the seventeenth century and the New Rome of the twenty-first. Replace Western Catholicism with Western democracy, and the colonial parallels are apparent: in both cases unguarded idealism leads to catastrophe. Interestingly, the theme was a favorite too of Graham Greene, to whom Endo has often been compared.

The Jesuit priest, William Johnston, translator of *Silence*, was not only a friend of Endo but administered the Last Rites to him. What was it that the novelist didn't like about Western Christianity? I once asked him. "Excessive clarity. Overabundance of logic," he replied. I wondered too about the "Japanese are unique" subtext in the author's thought. "Yes, he was very nationalist," he answered, "there's no doubt of that." Yet, though the young Endo saw irreconcilable differences between Japan and the West, in his last years he came to a more generous view, as reflected in his last novel, *Deep River* (1993). It explores the commonality of religions, and of all Endo's works it is the one that speaks to me most.

The title of the novel refers to the Ganges, India's mother river, and the book interweaves five different stories into the narrative flow. At its heart is the relationship of Mitsuko and Otsu, who studied together at college and who are reunited in Varanasi. She is a lost soul, cynical and empty; he is a renegade priest at odds with the Catholic Church. His spiritual journey has led him to the banks of the Ganges, where he helps the poor realize their dream of having their cremated ashes borne away by the river. Though still a Catholic, he has come to an Asian understanding of the divine: "God is not so much an existence as a force," he says, and he goes on to quote approvingly from Mahatma Gandhi:

> As a Hindu, I believe instinctively that there are varying degrees of truth in all religions. All religions spring from the same God. But every religion is imperfect. That is because they have all been transmitted by imperfect human beings. . . . There are many different religions, but they are merely various paths leading to the same place. . . . What difference does it make which of these separate paths we walk, so long as they all arrive at the same destination?

The book ends with Otsu's death and the rebirth of the cynical Mitsuko, almost as if she owes her transformation to his reincarnated spirit. In a visionary moment, she sees in the Ganges a "deep river" that runs through all humanity, a viewpoint that owes itself to the work of Carl Jung, of whom Endo was an admirer. The book ends with a spiritual affirmation that hovers delicately between Asian and Western concepts. "She did not know to whom she directed this manufactured prayer," runs the narrative. "Perhaps it was towards the Onion [a playful word that Otsu used for God]. Or perhaps it was towards something great and eternal that could not be limited to the Onion."

I was anxious to get Johnston's view of the novel, for it touches on themes that he has explored through his work with mysticism, or, as he prefers to call it, deep meditation. Was Endo at the end of his life reaching out beyond the confines of Christianity to embrace pluralism?

"Yes, I think so," he replied. "He said as much in an article he wrote, 'Futatsu no Mondai [Two Issues].' Don't forget that the Second Vatican Council talks of a 'Hidden Power' that is perceived by different people in different ways. In the novel Otsu says, 'God has many faces.' Endo was writing in that sense. Silence can help us realize that."

Afterwards I wondered if Johnston had meant silence, or *Silence*. Perhaps he meant both. Perhaps indeed Endo's title was not just referencing God's silence, but the notion that ultimate truth lies beyond words. It's an idea widely shared between religions, but no one put it better than the Chinese sage Lao Tzu: "He who knows does not speak; he who speaks does not know." At the deepest core of East and West, the twain surely do meet in a realm beyond words. In mysticism lies true oneness.

One mountain, many paths

One fine autumn day in 2010, Endo's *Deep River* came to mind as I found myself standing in front of Karematsu Jinja for a most unusual ceremony. Before me in the wooded grove, Catholics, Hidden Christians and Buddhists were assembled at the Shinto-style shrine for a ceremony that is held on November 3 every year. Initiated in 1999, it was intended as an act of reconciliation between groups that had been on bad terms since Meiji times. The year I attended—the eleventh in the series—the program featured an outdoor mass followed by a prayer recital by what was termed an "Old Christian" (no doubt the open nature of the event rendered "Hidden" meaningless).

Rows of seats had been set up in the clearing, in addition to which there were a good many people standing around or perched on rocks. In front of the shrine was a small choir, and to one side some eight priests discretely donned their vestments. Nuns and women in white head veils were prominent, while amateur photographers scurried among the trees and scrambled up an embankment for a better shot. The spontaneity together with the open-air setting gave the event a sense of immediacy. Outdoor worship has much to commend it, bringing one into direct contact with the living cosmos. Woods, it is said, were mankind's earliest temple: perhaps we should never have moved away.

For myself the focus of interest was the recital by Murakami Shigenori of Hidden Christian *orashio* (prayers). It was a remarkable occasion, for here was a descendant of people who had gathered illegally at this very spot to recite prayers taught to them by San Jiwan and Bastian. He faced towards the shrine, and as I listened to him I was struck by a sense of overhearing someone in private prayer. The solitary figure contrasted with the panoply of priests behind him: one represented a secret tradition nurtured among close-knit groups, the other a proselytizing Church with worldwide connections.

As Murakami went through his repertory of prayers, he referred occasionally to a book he held on his lap, which had been compiled in modern times. Transmission in the Edo period had been oral because of the need to avoid detection. Each generation of children was brought up to memorize the prayers, above all the eldest son on whose shoulders it fell to carry on the family tradition. When scholars came to study the prayers in modern times, they found those handed down in Japanese to be remarkably faithful, but those in Latin and Portuguese to have been corrupted. "Ave Maria gratia plena" had become "Abe Mariya hashiyabena." "Benedictus fructus" was transformed to "Bene-kentsu onha." Alarmingly, when questioned about the meaning of the prayers, the worshippers had absolutely no idea. Could anything be more absurd?

Looked at in another way, the Hidden Christian prayers actually make good sense. After all, it's as absurd to think God doesn't understand nonsense as it is to think he understands Latin or Portuguese. Rather than intelligibility, one would presume sincerity carries weight. Moreover, you don't have to look very far to find parallels to the Hidden Christian *orashio*, for ordinary Japanese have little understanding of Buddhist sutras. It's also worth noting that calls to reintroduce Latin to the Catholic mass are motivated precisely because the obsolete language is thought to provide a greater sense of mystery.

It's been suggested that Hidden Christian recitals are linked to the Shinto tradition of *kotodama* (word magic), by which the sound of a word has power in itself. It's a tradition shared by other ancient cultures, whereby the voicing of words has a very real effect, such that some are taboo and others used in a special formula for casting spells or curses. Similarly English speakers use abracadabra for its magical import, with little understanding of the origin or meaning. For Hidden Christians too, the meaningless prayers were imbued with a spiritual resonance, as if a special language to communicate with a God who passed all understanding.

Following the ceremony, I found myself talking with a Buddhist priest, who gave me to understand that his predecessors had helped protect the area's Hidden Christians. Really? I'd got the impression that Buddhist priests were keen to stamp out rivals and happy to collude with authorities.

"Maybe some did, but priests here knew of the Christians and felt sorry for them. They were poor, hardworking villagers.

They didn't harm anyone and they paid dues to the temple. The priest had to certify they were not Christian. Of course, maybe he suspected, but he didn't want to give them trouble. So he protected them. It was a kind of understanding. And you know, we Buddhists should show compassion!"

When we were joined by one of the organizers of the event, I asked how many Hidden Christians were still practicing in Sotome. "It's difficult to say," he told me. "There are two types: open and hidden. Those who are open are happy to talk about their practice. And they will invite people to rituals. Like Murakami-san who read the *orashio* today. But others don't like that. They want to practice in private, and they don't like outsiders to interfere. So even now they pretend they are not Kakure. Many are old now and don't want to change their ways. Maybe they are praying secretly at home and reciting *orashio*. Or maybe not," he said with a smile. "How can you know?"

One person who might know is Dorthoea Filius of Tokyo University, who has spent time studying present-day practitioners. She was struck by the amount of secrecy. Outsiders are shunned as intrusive. Marriage is within a closed circle of believers. There are no crosses to be seen, prayers are said in silence, and worship is addressed to the Buddhist Kannon or the Shinto *yama no kami* (mountain spirit). Holy objects are still secreted away in the depths of walls or roofs, for it is believed they will lose their force if seen by strangers. Like an esoteric cult in which salvation is restricted to the select, the practice is closely protected. Mystery is of the essence. For these Hidden Christians, being hidden is as much a part of their identity as being Christian.

The recital of *orashio* had been my main purpose in attending the Karematsu event, but my attention was unexpectedly seized by the address of the presiding priest. It was personal and unaffected, in keeping with the surrounds. Born on a Goto island, he could remember as a child hearing his grandmother recite prayers that he didn't fully understand. With four other family members he had celebrated a private Christmas at home, and his uncle had told him tales of Israel and Egypt, about which he wanted to hear more. Only at the age of ten did he realize that other believers celebrated on a different day and that his family was following a special kind of religion. Later, when he trained for the clergy, he learned Latin and realized the correct words of the Ave Maria prayer he'd memorized from his grandmother.

The confessional was clearly a means of reaching out to Hidden Christians, but I couldn't help wondering about the implications of having found the "true" faith. The priest concluded his talk by speaking of Sotome as his spiritual home, for it was from here that his family had originated before making the move to Goto some two hundred years earlier. I'd read of how the islands had been a refuge for Hidden Christians in times past, and my friend Christal Whelan had spent a year there researching the practice of present-day descendants. Sotome's seaside setting had given me a taste for more island adventure, and listening to the priest's talk in the autumn sunshine I made a sudden decision. Though I had been planning to head north, I changed direction to follow the flow of history. I knew I had got to go to Goto.

Chapter Ten

Sanctuary
(Goto Islands)

About sixty miles west of Nagasaki, set in the East China Sea, lies a group of 140 islands of which eighteen are inhabited. The archipelago has a population of some 60,000 and is situated at the extreme west of Japan proper (excluding Okinawa). It's as if the Hidden Christians were squeezed out to the very periphery of the country, as a consequence of which the islands have an unusual claim to fame: at 15 percent, Goto has the highest rate of Christians in Japan (virtually all Catholic). As you travel around the islands, you're struck by the number of churches. No fewer than fifty in all.

There are five main islands, hence the name (*Goto* means "five islands"). The largest is Fukuejima, and from Nagasaki a jetfoil takes just over an hour and a half to the main harbor. En route I kept wondering how long would it have taken in Edo times, for the islands are less sheltered than those of Amakusa and no doubt some of the small ships were blown off course. (Later I learned the average crossing took ten to twelve hours.) Now the only hardship is enduring the numbing engine throb in the jetfoil's stuffily enclosed cabin, where no blast of wind or spray of water ever enters.

At the harbor I met up with Matsubara-san, who had offered to guide me around the island. I'd been told it could be done in three hours but had opted for a more leisurely approach. I was soon glad I did, for our first stop was on a promontory in the kind of seaside setting that makes you want to spend time just breathing in the air. We were at Dozaki Church, an attractive redbrick building that stands down a secluded lane, facing towards the sea and surrounded by fields. It was the first church to be put up in the islands after the return of Catholicism in early Meiji times.

Looking around at the surroundings, I wondered about the community that the church had served. There were only a handful of houses and little sign of human activity; the lapping of waves was disturbed only by an occasional bird cry. But surely it wasn't for the peace that the site was chosen? "People came to the church by boat," Matsubara explained. "That's why it's facing the sea." One tends to forget just how important maritime travel was in Japan, even until relatively recently. In many places roads hardly existed: waterways were more important. It was the sea routes too that enabled the great influx of overseas people and cultures that molded ancient Japan.

Here, by the shore, Catholicism had been revived in Goto following toleration of Christianity in 1873, when an open-air mass was held. In lieu of a bell, people were summoned by conch shell. What an occasion it must have been, after the centuries of hiding and secrecy! The church was constructed in 1879, and in front of the building stands a statue of the man responsible, Father Maruman. Next to him is Father Pelu, who later rebuilt the church, and a third statue shows Johannes Goto, one of the 26 Martyrs crucified in Nagasaki. Pointing to him, Murakami asked me what I thought. I was somewhat at a loss: what after all can you say about a crucified body?

"Look at his legs," he said. "Don't you think they are very thick? Very tough?"

He had a point: the legs were rather solid looking.

"It's because he was from a peasant family. You see he joined the Christians, but he grew up in Goto. Goto peasants have to do hard work because the land is not productive. It is very hard to make a living. So from a young age they are working in the fields or at sea. They work long hours. Hard labor. You see?"

Near the statues were some Jizo rocks in the wayside manner one sees all over Japan. It was strange to find them in front of a church, and Matsubara explained that on their reverse, aged and barely discernible, were Christian images: a cross, Jesus and Mary. During ceremonies Hidden Christians had used them as a focus of worship, turning the stones around when they dispersed. In this way Jizo metamorphosed into Jesus, and back again.

In the 1970s Dozaki Church had been deemed redundant after a church was built nearby in a more suitable location for parishioners. There were plans to sell the building, but the authorities were persuaded otherwise; as it happened, I'd run into the priest responsible in Nagasaki. He'd been working in Goto at the time and successfully pleaded with the bishop to use the church as a museum. The only problem was that he had nothing to put in it! So he'd pressured his parishioners to look through their attics for heirlooms, and every weekend he'd scoured local villages for possible donations. Piece by piece, he'd put together a collection of two hundred items.

"You couldn't do that now," he told me. "People know too much about the value. Collectors come down from Tokyo and elsewhere. It's a business. It wasn't like that then. They were happy to donate things for free, because they wanted their family history to be preserved. But now if people find something in their house, maybe even just an ordinary object, they want to get money for it. They know there's a market for items like that."

Much of the Dozaki collection consists of artefacts handed down from the sixteenth and seventeenth centuries. Rosaries, medallions, sword guards, candleholders, bells, and pottery bearing crosses. A helpful notice points out something other museums are less eager to advertise: the *fumie* displayed are replica. (All the twenty-nine known originals are in Tokyo National Mu- seum: ten are wood, the rest metal.) There are too a number of Maria Kannon, and looking around the collection I was reminded of something a leading expert, Miyazaki Kentaro, had said to me as a warning about the number of fake exhibits in Hidden Christian museums. How can you tell the difference between a Kannon and a Maria Kannon, he asked? Answer: you can't. The only distinction is in the mind of the worshipper. But, whereas a statue of Kannon is commonplace and of little value, if it was worshipped two hundred years ago as Maria it would be a trea- sured item. As a result in modern times many ordinary statues were claimed as Hidden Christian; crosses had been added to Buddhist statues and counterfeits produced. It gives a whole new meaning to the phrase "false idol"!

One of the most intriguing items in the Dozaki collection is a mirror with a relief of Mary and Jesus on the reverse. From the front it appears purely practical, but when turned around it could be used for Hidden Christian purposes—like the worshippers, it had two faces. Mirrors are rich in symbolic and spiritual import, for they allow us to "reflect" on ourselves from a different angle, from the outside as it were. Interestingly, they stand at the heart of Shinto shrines, where they represent the soul of Amaterasu, though personally I see them as a powerful signifier of the divine within. Looking deep into their mirror, no doubt the Hidden Christians too, in their own way, saw the divine within.

Birth, death and resurrection

Following the museum visit I sat down with Matsubara-san to piece together the island history. Despite the remoteness, Chris- tianity had arrived relatively early, because of the proximity of the islands to Omura, where the connection to Europeans had proved advantageous. In 1566 missionaries were invited, and they arrived in the form of Luis de Almeida and an assistant named Lorenzo (the blind *biwa* player who played an important part in missionary work). Following a debate with Buddhists before 400 people, the daimyo had sided with the Christians in their championing of a Creator God. Shortly afterwards he fell ill, which the Buddhists were quick to suggest proved the falseness of the foreigners' faith. Japan's early history—as indeed that of other countries—has many such stories, when success of a deity was pinned on a single individual. On such slender threads hangs the fate of nations.

In this case the thread had a twist, for Almeida brought with him European medical skills and was able to treat the daimyo, following which he recovered. The physician-priest's success won renewed acclaim for his religion, and thereafter the faith was able to make ground with some 2,000 believers. Even the daimyo's wife and son converted. The Buddhist lobby remained powerful, however, and they pressured the daimyo to threaten his son with exile if he did not renounce Christianity. The young convert was adamant that he would rather choose exile than give up his faith. Later, when he succeeded his father, it must have seemed a Christian age was at hand, but policies at a national level had repercussions even here on these remote islands. Following Hideyoshi's Hakata edict in 1587, Goto's churches were destroyed. Ten years later the crucifixion of Johannes Goto proved a terrible warning.

The persecution of the seventeenth century apparently wiped out Christianity in Goto, and its revival came about in a curious way, through an influx of outsiders. Suffering from a shortage of income, the Goto daimyo realized his domain had reached the limits of production without substantial land development. For this he lacked manpower, and as it happened his neighbor in Omura had a surplus. Villagers were accordingly sent over from

Sotome where the land was relatively unproductive. A group of seventy had migrated as early as 1722, but the bulk came in the late 1790s when over 3,000 made the move from the mainland. They were Hidden Christians.

The population shift raises the intriguing possibility that the Omura daimyo knew just what he was doing. As long as the villagers were paying taxes, he may have turned a blind eye to their religion, yet should the central shogunate learn of their existence, there would be repercussions. He might therefore have taken advantage of the situation to export a potential problem. What did Matsubara think of the idea? "*Tabun*," he replied. "Maybe." Once I'd have pressed him for a clearer answer—"Yes or no?" Now, after long years in Japan, I was happy to accept the vagueness and the implied modesty. Opinionated views are not the Japanese way.

One imagines the Sotome migrants had expectations of a better life. Go west, they were ordered, and they set off in boats for a new world that was pitched as a land of opportunity. Yet things did not turn out that way, for as newcomers they were shunned by resentful residents and consigned to the bottom of the pecking order. Instead of finding prosperity, they were given isolated and barren patches of land. Integration was hindered by their clannishness: anxious to protect their secret, they not only kept to themselves but married among their own kind too. The result was a segregated existence in which the despised mainlanders had to fend as best they could, while pinning their hopes on a better life in the world to come.

Practice, not theory

In religious terms, the situation of the Hidden Christians was stark. For the most part illiterate, they had no priests, no Bible and no contact with the organized church. The absence of documents makes it difficult to know exactly how they practiced their faith, but one thing seems clear: even at the outset some had only a hazy idea of the religion, for it was inherited from parents who had on average just seven to ten days of instruction. Breadth over depth had been the Jesuit policy, and the consequence was converts who barely understood the complexities of their faith. The ratio of priests to believers in 1614 had been 1 to 3,061. In 1579, it had been as high as 1 to 5,652. As a result, the workload was overwhelming, and Father Organtino in 1589 is recorded as hearing 3,500 confessions in a year. If you work out the mathematics, it comes to almost ten every single day—and that's on top of his other duties and the time necessary for traveling.

The paucity of priests, as we have seen, meant that believers were used to operating on their own, through self-help organizations such as confraternities and prayer groups. On the other hand, the shortage of instruction meant that Christian concepts were often poorly understood or simply equated to Japanese beliefs. Before going to Goto, I'd attended a talk by Higashibaba Ikuo of Tenri University, who explained that the Catholicism inherited by the Hidden Christians was never orthodox in the first place, but filtered through a Japanese consciousness. Sin was equated with *tsumi* (Shinto "pollution"), which required purification. Rosaries and crosses were treated as *omamori* (charms). Scourging was seen as a form of austerity to gain spiritual merit, and ritual was treated as an end in itself, independent of doctrine. The situation was typified by an incident described by Luis Frois, who wrote of a convert found praying with Buddhist beads despite having a rosary by his side. When asked why, he replied:

> "Padre, I have been a very sinful person, and I prayed with Christian beads, asking our Lord to have mercy for my soul. In a sermon, however, I learned that the Lord is very strict in his judgment. Since my sin is so

great, I may not deserve the glory of Deus. I am therefore paying to Amida Buddha too so that I will be able
to go to the Pure Land in case I cannot go to heaven."

Bereft of priests, Hidden Christians were unable to observe
Catholicism's seven sacraments with one notable exception:
baptism. The Council of Trent (1545–63) had stressed its role
in ensuring salvation and that, in the absence of priests, quali-
fied lay people could perform the ritual. Since baptism was their
sole sacrament, Hidden Christians ascribed it special significance
and the person in charge was awarded high status. It was readily
adapted in Japan, because of a tradition of holy water: in Shinto
it is used as a purifying agent and in esoteric Buddhism to signify
passing into the highest stage (*kanjo*).

To avoid suspicion, Hidden Christians gatherings were small
in number. They were also largely male (officeholders were restricted to men). Rituals generally proceeded in three parts. First,
offerings were made, together with an explanation of the meeting's
purpose. Then came prayers and whatever ritual was being celebrated. Finally there was communal eating. Anyone familiar with
Shinto ritual will recognize the tripartite nature, which is standard procedure in shrine ceremonies. The *naorai* or communal
eating is a means of deepening group bonds as well as a symbolic sharing of food with the *kami*. In this way it's both a spiritual and a social communion: there's a vertical connection to a
higher spirit, and a horizontal connection with fellow believers.

The heart of Hidden Christian practice was the recital of
memorized prayers. The Lord's Prayer and the Hail Mary were
standard, as was the Latin version of the Hail Mary known as
Ave Maria. One prayer had particular significance, however: the
Konchirisan (Contrition). In a sense, it was a Hidden Christian
lifeline, for their whole existence was in contravention of Church
teaching. Instead of being faithful to the word of God, they

trod on the *fumie* every year, registered with Buddhist temples, made written assurances of conversion, and took a certificate of membership. They even held Buddhist funerals. The sense of guilt felt about all this needed to be assuaged, and contrition was the means.

A section on contrition had been included in the *Dochirina Kirishitan*, in addition to which Luis Cerqueira had published a *Short Treatise on Perfect Contrition (Konchirisan no Ryaku)* in 1603. It was transmitted orally, and some written copies were handed down too. The central tenet was that God, being compassionate, would forgive those who showed the proper form of repentance. It was not enough to simply say the prayer of contrition, but one had to be sincere and atone for one's sin. The prayer also substituted for confession, which missionaries had taught was necessary to win salvation. In this way, it became a vital means of self-help in a situation where there was no priestly forgiveness. Through contrition, the Hidden Christians could forgive themselves.

Syncretism

As elsewhere, the Hidden Christians of Goto lived in isolated communities and had little if any contact with other groups. The autonomy meant that villagers could act as a self-supporting unit, independent of outsiders. In this way it strengthened solidarity and helped subvert Tokugawa control mechanisms such as the collective responsibility system of the *goningumi* (groups of five households). On the other hand, free of central supervision the isolated groups developed their own idiosyncratic customs. Even between neighboring villages there could be small differences, while regional groupings varied considerably. Some remained relatively faithful to the original teachings, but, as we have seen, others integrated Japanese elements.

The drive to syncretism was initiated at an early stage by a culling process in which those most versed in Catholicism became martyrs, while survivors, by definition, were more inclined to compromise. It's worth noting that the majority of educated Christians—samurai and nobles—gave up their religion, whereas those who went underground were largely unlettered peasants and artisans. As a consequence, the Hidden Christian communities came to "Japanize" their religion, as if in the absence of European instruction they were reverting to default mode. The Buddhist and Shinto camouflage adapted out of necessity in the early years became fully integrated into the religion. Rather than acting as a substitute, Amida got equal billing with Deus.

One of the ways in which the European religion was indigenized was through adoption of the hereditary principle, so that eldest sons inherited the offices of their fathers. In this way, continuity was institutionalized and ancestors honored. Other examples of syncretism included ceremonies to purify homes, taboo days, and the use of sashimi and saké in place of bread and wine. Martyrs were treated as *kami* with otherworldly powers, none more so than Bastian. The dead in Goto were presented with a piece of cloth from "Bastian's kimono" to ensure entry into the next world, and a piece of camellia was placed in coffins following a tradition that the calendar maker had miraculously carved a cross into such a tree with his finger.

The only Hidden Christian text to have survived from Edo times is a curious document entitled *Tenchi Hajime no Koto*, translated by Christal Whelan as *The Beginnings of Heaven and Earth*. Just thirty pages long, it reads like a collection of folk stories loosely based on the Bible. Creation, the fall of Man, the flood, the miraculous birth of Jesus, his retreat to do austerities, the betrayal by a follower, and the crucifixion form the core of the work, onto which are strung Japanese elements to make the stories more relevant to their audience. As such it's a wonderful example of how tales evolve during transmission, taking on characteristics of the local culture. Middle Eastern myths given a European glossing are here filtered through a Far Eastern consciousness. Noah's flood becomes a tsunami. The Virgin Mary is a twelve-year-old girl from the Philippines. The three kings come from Turkey, Mexico and France.

Whelan speculates that the authorship is collective, and that the text originated in Sotome before being taken to Goto. It's possible the stories were handed down from blind *biwa* storytellers, which would mean they represent a form of folk entertainment as much as religious instruction. (Often compared with Homer and the Greek tradition, the storytellers were responsible for transmitting the epic *Tale of Heike*.) Some of the most striking oddities are simple matters of transmission. The crucifixion is arranged by two men called Ponsha and Piroto. Eve doesn't eat an apple (unknown in Japan at the time) but a persimmon-like fruit called *macan*. Other changes, however, show interference from the Japanese mindset, or "mudswamp" as Endo calls it. The Trinity, for example, comprises Deus, his son and Mary. It bears out the author's thesis about the inclinations of the Japanese to sanctify the maternal.

Some of the passages bring to mind the mythology of the eighth-century *Kojiki*, Japan's oldest chronicle, in that they explain the origin of Japanese customs. In one episode, Deus gives humans rice as a divine gift, and in another the Ave Maria is explained as a prayer composed at the Abe River! One sees too the influence of Japanese tradition in the emphasis on the vitalizing nature of water. Prominence is given to the first bath of Jesus after birth, and to Mary's bathwater being used to heal a sick child. When it comes to his baptism, Jesus divides the water into 40,000 rivers so that there'll be enough for all mankind. Rather than a symbolic agent, water is here treated as the gift of a beneficent God in keeping with the belief system of Shinto, in which gratitude for its nourishing and purifying qualities plays an important part.

Buddhism too has a significant place in the text: indeed, it seems at times to be equated with Christianity. "As for the one you worship as a Buddha, he is called Deusu, Lord of Heaven," runs the text. Those who are baptised are promised entry to paradise, where, curiously, it is guaranteed that they will become buddhas. It recalls the early days of the mission, when priests were presumed to be preaching a variant of Buddhism, and as late as 1648 a Zen monk wrote an anti-Christian book in which he maintained that Jesus had simply misunderstood Buddha's message. It's not such an outrageous idea: only the other day I happened to hear a podcast of the late great Alan Watts talking about Jesus in terms of an awakened being whose essential message of compassion and salvation was not dissimilar from that of the Buddha. Perhaps in their own way the Hidden Christians had stumbled on a deeper truth!

The End Time

After our visit to Dozaki Church, Matsubara and I went on a tour of Fukuejima. In temporal terms it took us to the end of the Tokugawa shogunate, when regime change ushered in an emperor-centered system. Yet instead of the bright dawn of a new age, Goto's Hidden Christians had found themselves subject to renewed persecution from a nationalistic government determined to show its strength by standing up to the West.

"You see this space here," said Matsubara, pointing to a carpet. We were in a church called Roya no Sako, and the carpet was about 180 square feet. "Here was what we call Crowded Hell. Almost two hundred people, including children, were squashed into this space for eight months. Can you imagine? There was not even space to sit or lie. More than forty people died. You can see their names over there," he said pointing at a memorial. Along with the names were the poignant last words of a twelve-year-old girl. "Mother, father, goodbye," she told them, "Now I'm going to paradise."

Afterwards, we took the ferry to the largest island in the Upper Goto grouping, called Nakadori. First we drove up through well-cultivated land to the northern part of the island where Goto airport is located. Here, in 1867, a Catholic named Domingo Mori Matsujiro had started a school at his residence with the collusion of a French priest. The convert was self-taught and familiar with Dutch learning, and his home became the focus for Hidden Christians fleeing persecution. Now the site is marked by a church, built in 1919 by parishioners who quarried the stone and built it themselves. It's a charming building, but sadly it's used just once a month these days for want of a congregation. As elsewhere, young people left the area in the 1950s in search of work and the community died out. It's said those who return for the monthly service are motivated by the effort their ancestors took in creating the church.

The persecution that hit Kashiragajima was part of a clampdown felt all over Goto. It led to an incident in 1873 involving a Kirishitan cave where a small group had gone into hiding. The cave lies beneath a cliff on the southern promontory of the small Wakamatsu Island and is accessible only by sea. Before it stands a statue of the crucified Christ, put up in 1967, and the image is used in tourist brochures for its picturesque quality: sparkling blue sea, rocky shoreline, and a solitary figure in pure white. Matsubara knew a fisherman who would take us there, and I was delighted at the prospect of fresh air and island scenery. Even more so when Matsubara revealed the boat owner was from a Hidden Christian family.

For a while, we moved through the kind of enclosed waters you get in the Inland Sea, where green-fringed islands are dispersed in pleasing patterns, and I took advantage of the occasion to ask our captain about his family. He said he remembered his grandparents reciting prayers but didn't think much about it. His parents had inherited items such as a small clay figure thought to be Jesus, "but I'm not interested in all that," he said with a laugh. "I'm a bad Christian." He was a good sailor though, for he knew the coastline well enough to skirt close to underwater rocks that loomed frighteningly large by the boat's side.

It wasn't long before we rounded the promontory to find ourselves in wide open water and exposed to the sea's buffeting. Up ahead I could see the statue of Christ on the rocks and wondered how we were going to land. Alarmingly the captain steered us straight up the rocky shoreline, squashing the tires attached to the front of the boat until the prow rested by a shelf-like rock onto which we alighted. The cave entrance can't be seen from the sea, and I was expecting something small and cramped. It turned out to be a surprisingly spacious cavern, some hundred and fifty feet in length and fifteen feet wide. Though it was a bright sunny day, inside it was dark and damp despite the openings on three of the sides. Here at the beginning of Meiji times a small band of Hidden Christians had lived, the sea their only companion.

According to Matsubara, the group had not stayed the whole time in the cave but went up to open land on the cliffs above, descending to the hiding place in times of danger. Some of the huge boulders were large enough to lie on, and I tried one out. The hard rough edges cut into my back, while underneath the incoming tide made strange gurgling sounds as it washed against the beach. It would hardly make for a comfortable night. On one of the walls was a shelf-like structure that looked custom-made for an altar, near which a natural chimney flue led up to a small opening in the roof of the cave high above. It was this that proved the group's downfall, for smoke from their cooking was noticed by officials crossing from Kyushu, and troops were dispatched to round them up. They were arrested, sent to jail and executed.

On the return trip I asked our captain about the markings inside the cave, but he laughingly said he had never been inside. The lack of curiosity surprised me. Perhaps as a local he took his surrounds for granted, or perhaps it showed rejection of his parents' religion. He told me, though, that a group of people from a church nearby gather every month at a rock before the cave to celebrate the memory of those who perished. It had been a sanctuary in a group of islands that were themselves a kind of refuge from the mainland. Yet even here on the uninhabited shore of a remote island within the country's most westerly territory, the hawk-like eye and ruthless arm of the state had managed to penetrate. Such was the hostility towards Christians.

Past and present

Afterwards, Matsubara and I went to visit Kiri Church. It stands white and proud on a small hill overlooking narrow straits, like a beneficent guardian keeping watch over the ebb and flow below. We had hoped to talk to the parish priest, but he was away and instead we came across an elderly nun cleaning his house. She gave us a tour of the church, but its plain interior was disappointing and failed to match the grandeur of the setting. There wasn't even any stained glass to offset the bare walls, for which the nun apologized. "People always say the view here is beautiful, but they never say that of the church," she said with a rueful smile.

She told us that about twenty people attended service every morning, and about fifty on Sundays. Realizing our interest in Hidden Christians, she pointed down to a group of houses on the other side of the narrow strait.

"You see the houses over there. The people who live in them are 'Hidden.' Actually, we call them 'Separated Christians.' They refuse to come to church, saying they don't want to change their ways. It's too troublesome for them, maybe. And they want to keep the faith of their parents. You know they came over to Goto two hundred years ago, but they were not treated well. They were a kind of outsider. And people looked down on them. Many have names with the kanji for 'down' in them, like Shimoda, Shimomura or Yamashita. The leader of the group in the cave you visited was Yamashita Yonosuke."

I asked her about the relationship of the "Separated Christians" with the church, since they lived in such close proximity, and whether there was any contact at all.

"Yes, we told them they are on the wrong path and that they should come back to the Church where their ancestors started. They have no confession. We said they should join with us and follow the proper way, but they don't want to listen. But do you know what's interesting? They call the priest when they are going to die for the last rites. They say that's enough for them."

What did the nun think of that, I wondered? "It's for them to decide," she told me. Then added, "But I think they're wrong."

Afterwards, I asked Matsubara-san to accompany me to the village to see if we could strike up a conversation. I knew the villagers would be wary of outsiders but thought the presence of a local might be reassuring. We found an elderly woman tending to vegetables on a small plot, but our inquiries were met with pleasant evasions. Matsubara asked her something about the "old calendar people," but she waved her hand in a dismissive manner to signify she didn't know anything about all that. I'd been warned that they liked to keep their religion private, which is understandable. These days it's said the Hidden Christians are no longer in hiding from persecution, but from journalists and researchers that descend on them in droves.

One person who managed to breach the wall of reserve is Christal Whelan, following a year-long stay on the island of Narushima in Lower Goto. The result was a remarkable documentary called *Otaiya* (the Hidden Christian name for Christmas). The island once had a strong Hidden Christian community comprising the majority of the population, but migration and modernization in the 1950s led to the tradition being shunned by the younger generation. Baptisms came to a stop in 1992, and as a result the religion became the preserve of the elderly. When Whelan filmed in 1996, it was on its last legs. Literally. The two Hidden Christian leaders featured in her documentary were in their nineties, one ninety-nine and the other ninety-two.

The two men (referred to as priests) celebrate separately because of a clash of traditions: for one of them the day is fixed as December 23, for the other it is December 24. It's indicative of the differences even between villages on a small island. The older of the priests performs the ritual on his own for want of fellow practitioners, and sets out empty plates for two missing officeholders. The other priest breaks tradition by leaving his village to celebrate with others. As well as the recital of *orashio* prayers, there is a form of Mass in which rice and saké substitute for the host and wine. The precision with which the priests lay out their dishes reflects a concern with form astonishing for men in their nineties. Just as remarkably, the priests are able to recite from memory, testimony to how firmly their minds must have been trained when young.

When Whelan made her documentary, she found little awareness or interest in orthodox Christian beliefs such as the story of Jesus. More important was maintaining family tradition. Endo's "mudswamp" had transformed the religion into something very Japanese, where form was more important than content and ancestor worship outweighed belief. Curiously, while watching Whelan's documentary, I was struck most of all by the manner of eating. Mimicking the style of the Eucharist, the ritual rice was eaten from the palm of the hand rather than with chopsticks. It was shockingly un-Japanese, and there was something in licking off the remains from the hand that reminded me of the customs of "Southern Barbarians." Japanese manners by contrast can transform the function of eating into a pleasing ritual in itself, a trait that is reflected in the wider culture, where one often gets the feeling that aesthetics matter more than ethics.

Before departing Kiri Church, Matsubara and I inspected the statues that stand in front of the building. They showed three Hidden Christians pointing excitedly towards Nagasaki, where reports had come in 1865 of a Christian church and a Catholic priest. After almost two hundred and sixty years of isolation, it must have seemed unbelievable. I'd gone to Goto to get to know the Edo-era retreat, but now I wanted to explore in more depth the historic transition in early Meiji times from persecution to toleration. How had it come about, and why? In Nagasaki lay a district called Urakami that had once been a Hidden Christian stronghold and where the chief historic events of these years had taken place. It was there that I was headed, and while I wanted to focus on the remarkable incidents of 1865, it would give me a chance to recap what had happened to the Catholics in Nagasaki during the years of persecution. After all, the town had been key to developments ever since its emergence in the 1570s.

Chapter Eleven

Revelation
(Urakami)

The Dutch at Dejima

Nagasaki was once known as "Little Rome" for its concentration of Catholic power, and long after the full force of the persecution had been unleashed, it remained the toughest nut for authorities to crack. In the years following the 1614 ban, churches were torn down and Shinto shrines or Buddhist temples erected in their stead. It reversed the previous Christianization of so-called pagan sites: the uncompleted San Francisco Church was turned into a prison, and on the site of the demolished San Juan Bautista Church a Nichiren temple called Honrei-ji was put up. The Zen temple of Shuntoku-ji, erected in 1640 on the site of a former church, houses a well in which it's said that even now can be heard the cries of martyred Christians.

The city's most prestigious shrine, Suwa Jinja, also dates from this time. It was founded in the 1620s, though it was only in 1641 that it moved to its present location on a small hill with commanding views. The climb up the two hundred stone steps is steep but worth it, for in addition to the panorama of town and bay are some unexpected curiosities. One is a bust of the French naval officer Pierre Loti, who wrote *Madame Chrysanthème*

(1887), precursor of *Madame Butterfly*. There are rumors too that a Christian statue from a ruined church might have been used as a *goshintai* (spirit body) for one of the *kami* enshrined. If so, it would be a remarkable example of Shinto's ability to incorporate alien elements.

From a conversation with one of the priests, I gathered that the shrine had aroused opposition when it was first built and that it had worked hard to win the affection of the populace. One of the means was a popular ritual in which a priest possessed by a *kami* plunged his hand shaman-style into boiling water (nowadays bamboo is used instead of a hand). Registration at the shrine was made compulsory, and in the 1630s a great autumn festival called the Kunchi Matsuri was launched, which gave an opportunity to root out Hidden Christians who were loathe to participate. Held from October 7 to 9 each year, it became a showcase event and is considered now to be one of the "big three festivals" of Japan. Even the Dutch, exceptionally, were allowed off the artificial island of Dejima to attend.

Created in 1636 by digging across a small promontory, Dejima was a fan-shaped island created for the Portuguese. Following their expulsion, the Dutch were moved there in 1641, and for over 200 years they remained the only Westerners allowed to do trade with Japan (the Chinese also traded from Nagasaki). It must have been a strange existence for the twelve to twenty Europeans (the Dutch occasionally employed others, such as Germans). Living on the island with them were servants from Indonesia or Africa, together with Japanese officials, guards and paramours, all cooped up in a community of three streets and some forty buildings. The longest side of the island was 620 feet, the shortest just 230: in all, it was about one-third the size of the Tokyo Dome. It's hard to imagine what it must have felt like, though one person who has done so with panache is novelist David Mitchell in *The Thousand Autumns of Jacob de Zoet* (2010).

Only a thin stretch of water separated Dejima from the mainland, and the small connecting bridge was guarded at both ends. Profits were good in the early years, when there was an average of seven ships a year (the number was later restricted to two). The main export was silver, with copper, camphor, porcelain and lacquer goods prominent among the other items. Imports included Asian fabrics, particularly raw silk, as well as European goods like the books and scientific equipment that in the eighteenth century stimulated the influential *rangaku* (Dutch learning).

The first time I visited Nagasaki, I was on my way to meet a friend when the tram drew up at a stop named Dejima. Out of the window I could see a handful of Western buildings with an entrance where people were paying to get in. Intrigued, I got off at the next stop and walked back, away from the roaring traffic and into a reconstructed slice of European seclusion within an isolated Japan. The land was reclaimed in Meiji times and incorporated into the city, but the rebuilt street gives a fascinating glimpse into the self-enclosed world of an earlier age. Some of the residences and warehouses contain a detailed account of the activities that went on there.

At one end of the street stands a huge weighing scale, the whole raison d'être of an island dedicated to trade. At the other end is a vegetable garden where European legumes are grown, as they were in the past. There are exotic farm animals too, such as pigs, goats and cows. Given the limited acreage, the house of the Chief Factor (as the head of the station was called) is surprisingly spacious, with a four-poster bed and full-sized billiard table. For Japanese of the time, the island was a source of fascination, and artists were fond of portraying the Europeans dressed in their finery with African slaves in attendance. The guide told me there are plans to make a complete reconstruction, with waterways that mimic the original. Perhaps, as at the theme park Huis Ten Bosch, you'll be able to stay overnight and go Dutch.

The privileged position of the Europeans derived not only from their anti-Catholic credentials as shown during the Shimabara revolt, but from a willingness to disavow all ties to Christianity. No Bibles or services were allowed on Dejima. It meant too submitting to exhaustive searches by the Japanese, who looked for Christian literature and firearms—two equally explosive substances as far as the Tokugawa were concerned. In return for their trade monopoly, the Dutch were expected to show vassal status through an annual journey to Edo where they prostrated themselves before the shogun. On at least one occasion they literally danced for him.

Every year the Dutch were required to go through the ritual of *fumie,* reports of which circulated around Europe. One of those to take exception was the cleric Jonathan Swift, who took a dig at them in *Gulliver's Travels* (1726). Japan is the only real country among the fantasy lands visited by the titular hero, and after being stranded on its coast he is taken to the capital at Edo to see "the emperor" (like others, Swift misunderstood the ruling structure). During the audience Gulliver pretends to be a Dutchman so as to get to Dejima and return to Europe.

> I therefore most humbly entreated his royal favor to give order that I should be conducted in safety to Nangasac [Nagasaki]. To this I added another petition that for the sake of my patron the king of Luggnagg, his majesty would condescend to excuse me performing the ceremony imposed on my countrymen of trampling upon the crucifix. When this latter petition was interpreted to the emperor, he seemed a little surprised; and said, He believed I was the first of my countrymen who ever made any scruple in this point; and then he began to doubt whether I was a real Hollander or not; but rather suspected I must be a Christian.

No doubt Swift had a good chuckle to himself at this slight on the Dutch. Thereafter Gulliver proceeds to "Nangasac" by grace of the emperor's friendship with the king of Luggnagg, from where he catches a boat to Amsterdam. Though he is questioned about whether he has trampled on the *fumie*, he cunningly evades answering by saying that he has satisfied the emperor in all particulars. In this way he leaves Japan with his honor unsullied, unlike the miserable Dutch.

Swift's account takes us well into the age of isolation, decades after 1644, when the last known missionary was executed. Yet authorities continued to be vigilant, paranoid even. In 1680 when Tokugawa Tsuneyoshi came to power, he took exception to the fact that one of the characters used to write "Kirishitan" was the same as that in his given name, so he ordered a new spelling for the religion that retained the phonetic sound but read: "cut the limbs till they bleed." It was symptomatic of the contempt with which the faith was regarded. All incoming ships were searched for any trace of seditious literature, much like Soviet commissars looking for evidence of Western decadence. In 1695 a junk from China was found to be importing a twenty-eight-volume encyclopedia containing an entry for Father Ricci (1552–1610), one of the founding fathers of the China mission. Not only was the offending volume seized, but the entire junk was put into quarantine, meaning the crew could not go on shore for food. Imagine their bewilderment: the poor sailors probably had no idea about Christianity!

In 1708 an Italian missionary named Giovanni Battista Sidotti (1667–1714) took a boat from the Philippines and had himself dropped off in Kyushu. Exactly what the quixotic priest was thinking is hard to imagine. He was quickly apprehended and taken to the Kirishitan jail in Edo, which for want of Christians had been holding common criminals. No doubt, like their modern counterparts, the interrogators wanted to know what foreign power had put the priest up to his suicidal venture. According to reports, he resisted all threats and even managed to convert the elderly couple caring for him. As punishment he was put in a hole in the ground and for years kept alive on starvation rations. Following his death, the Kirishitan jail reverted to holding ordinary criminals, until in 1792 it was abolished along with the office of religious prosecution. There simply were no Christians left. Or so it was thought.

Coming out

In 1831, the Paris Foreign Mission Society was entrusted with responsibility for spreading Catholicism to Japan and Korea. The Portuguese had dominated the sixteenth century; now it was the turn of the French. So eager were they to get to work that one of the missionaries went to the nominally independent Okinawa in 1844 to learn Japanese. He was joined there in 1855 by Father Prudence Girard, who belying his first name journeyed to the Far Eastern frontier as soon as Commodore Perry's handful of Black Ships had successfully pried open Japan's closed doors. In 1857 the Harris Treaty permitted Americans in Japan the right to practice their religion. Given the aversion to Christianity, it was a demonstration of Western power. Others were eager for parity, and in 1859 the French signed a similar treaty. Who should be their translator? None other than Father Prudence Girard. It was as if the days of Rodrigues and the priest-interpreter had returned all over again.

By the end of the 1850s there were several treaty ports in Japan, and the foreign enclaves were served by Christian priests. The first to secure a chapel was Hakodate in 1860, with Yokohama getting a church a year later. By the end of 1864 Nagasaki also had one, the first to be built in the city since the heady days of the early seventeenth century. It stood on the side of Oura Hill at the top of which the Scottish merchant Thomas Glover had built a splendid mansion the year before. Called Oura Tenshudo (Hall of the Lord of Heaven), the church was a wooden building with stained glass, the construction of which was supervised by Father Bernard Petitjean (1828–84) who had arrived in Japan four years earlier. It faced towards Nishizaki Hill, where the 26 Martyrs had been crucified, and in February 1865 it was formally dedicated to their memory.

A month after the dedication, Petitjean noticed a group of Japanese loitering near the church. It was unusual, for conversion to Christianity remained a capital offense. The ban on the European religion was one of the very few policies to be unmodified throughout the Tokugawa period, as if it were the very rationale on which the hermetic state was built. The anti-Christian policy united different sections of society; like the threat of capitalism for the Soviet Union, it was used as justification for draconian powers by an authoritarian regime.

Intrigued by the group of Japanese, Petitjean went over to the church and to his surprise was followed inside. An even bigger surprise ensued, as he described the next day in a letter to a friend:

> At about a quarter past noon yesterday I saw a group of some 15 Japanese men and women standing in front of the gate. As I opened the church door and approached the altar, the group followed me. A woman aged 40–50 came closer to me, placing her hand on her chest and said, "All of us here have the same heart as you." "Really?" I asked the woman, "then where are you from?" "From Urakami," said she. "All of us in Urakami have the same heart as you." And a question followed, "Where is the statue of Santa Maria?" Santa Maria! Little did I doubt on hearing this holy name.

Those Japanese people must be the descendants of
Japanese Christians from long ago.

Urakami was a valley a mile to the north, which contained
a few scattered settlements. The area had been donated to the
Jesuits by Arima Harunobu after he defeated a rival with the help
of Portuguese weapons, and the missionaries had built a small
hospital there for lepers, part of a policy of proselytizing by good
works rather than politics. In 1588 Hideyoshi had confiscated
the area, together with Nagasaki, and placed it under control of
the central government. When the clampdown on Christianity
began in 1614, people in the city were exposed to the full force
of persecution, whereas outlying areas like Urakami escaped
with less scrutiny. It thus proved a safe haven for those who were
believers, particularly after the Shimabara Uprising of 1638. It
was their descendants who approached Father Petitjean over two
hundred years later.

In the following weeks, the French priest became aware of
over a thousand more believers in the Urakami valley, together
with an equal number in the surrounding hills. Given the dangers involved, both sides had to proceed with caution. For their
part, the Hidden Christians were nervous about revealing
themselves and anxious to check the credentials of the foreigner.
Did he belong to "the great chief of the Kingdom of Rome?"
Was he celibate? Had he arrived in a black ship? Only after re-
ceiving satisfactory answers could they really believe that the
prophecies of Bastian had finally come true. (As in Goto and
Sotome, the Hidden Christians of the area treasured the memory of the martyr.)

When news of all this reached Pope Pius IX, he declared it
"the miracle of the Orient." In the long history of the Church,
here was one of the most extraordinary developments: the faith
had been handed down orally by generations of illiterate peas-

ants without recourse to priests or Bible. Yet after the initial excitement, Petitjean and his colleagues became concerned to what extent the villagers really were Catholic. The Church had strict teachings on the subject, for in 1715 Pope Clement had ruled that Chinese Rites were not acceptable for Church members, which by implication meant native practices elsewhere. Yet the Hidden Christians had integrated many Japanese customs. They had no proper sacraments, except for baptism; they had no authentic texts; and they had some very strange beliefs and practices indeed.

A month after the initial contact, Petitjean met with a Hidden Christian baptiser from Urakami, who gave him a copy of *Tenchi Hajimari no Koto*. It had been written down from memory in the early nineteenth century, and Petitjean thought it a reasonably accurate account of the Bible given the circumstances. If so, it may have been different from the Goto version, though we will never know for sure: ironically, it was destroyed by fire in 1874 after being sent for safekeeping to Yokohama.

Church visit

Anyone interested in the history of this time will naturally head for Oura Church, where the initial encounter of official and proto-Catholics took place. It is the only Western-style building in the country to be designated a national treasure and one of Nagasaki's premier attractions. The original structure was enlarged in 1879 and rebuilt after World War Two, when it suffered damage. With its white walls and palm trees it has a southern European feel, enhanced by the hillside setting. The church is given over now to tourism (a building nearby serves for religious occasions), and halfway up the stone staircase is a relief depicting a robed Petitjean. Bible in hand and arms outstretched, he towers over a group of Japanese kneeling before a statue of the

Madonna. The first of the women is turned inquiringly towards the priest, while the others look towards the statue with rapt devotion. It was Maria, not Jesus, they were eager to see.

Inside the church stands the very statue. It's a surprisingly colorful affair, with Mary clothed in a green robe over a red underskirt, not unlike a kimono in style. The golden dress patterns are set off by a headdress that looks for all the world like an imperial crown, and to her chest she clutches the baby Jesus. With her serene expression, she looks down on those below with a regal beauty—a true symbol of the Mother made divine. Like nature itself, she gave birth in miraculous fashion. Robed in Western garb, she's a modern Earth Goddess who speaks of the mystery of creation.

Alongside the church is a small museum of Hidden Christian artifacts, housed in a Latin Divinity School built by Father Petitjean in 1875. The wooden rooms only have space for a few simple items: a Maria Kannon; a scourge; Spanish medallions; a Bastian calendar with days marked as to whether meat could be eaten; and a copy of the *Konchirisan* (prayer of contrition) that the Hidden Christians held so dear. One of the displays explains the four strategies by which believers protected their faith:

1. In order not to be arrested, escape from Nagasaki to Goto and other remote places.
2. As in Urakami and Imamura, everyone pretended to be Buddhists and handed down their beliefs by creating an organization in which such people played key roles such as the *choukata*, who protected the secret teachings, *mizukata* who did baptisms, and *kurikata* who transmitted the calendar year.
3. For worship they used disguised statues and images, such as the Maria Kannon and "closet gods" which looked Buddhist or Shinto.

4. At the beginning they couldn't bring themselves to step on the *fumie*. But gradually they were able to manage it. Afterwards they offered a prayer of contrition (*Konchirisan*) or did penance.

The strategies served the Hidden Christians well. Did the authorities turn a blind eye to them? It seems probable, for as long as they kept to themselves and paid their tax, the illiterate peasants hardly constituted a threat. Occasionally attention would be drawn to them, which led to a round of persecution known by believers as *kuzure*, or "collapse." The first to hit Urakami was from 1790 to 1795, the second in 1842. There were arrests but no executions. A third round in 1859 resulted in ten people dying under torture. The fourth proved the most severe of all and took place in the years following the meeting with Petitjean, when a new government had taken charge and the country stood on the threshold of Westernization. The timing was unfortunate, in more than one sense.

The fourth persecution

As word spread about the French priest in Nagasaki, Hidden Christians across the region chose to disclose their existence. One such group was from Goto, others came from Omura. The activities around Oura Church alarmed the authorities, and warnings were issued. Petitjean and his colleagues took to wearing disguise and operating under cover of dark, just as priests had done 240 years earlier. Anxious to reintroduce the villagers to the Church, they set about giving instruction. It was a clear violation of the foreign power treaties, but with Japan in political crisis, Westerners were beginning to flex their muscles.

In 1867 a batch of fifteen French priests arrived in Japan. They were of a different breed to their Portuguese predecessors, less accommodating and more concerned with doctrinal purity. Villagers were not only urged to give up syncretic practices such as the worship of Maria Kannon but encouraged to stop holding Buddhist funerals. Led by the priests, they set up four small chapels for worship—a radical departure from the secrecy of private houses. The intention was to pressure authorities into acceptance; it proved a fatal mistake.

A local farmer took it upon himself to pen a letter to the village headman stating his refusal to hold a Buddhist funeral, which was passed on to Nagasaki prosecutors. Troops entered Urakami, there were confiscations, 64 arrests, and one of the chapels was destroyed. A French priest visiting the area had to flee for the hills. Investigations followed, and pretty soon 100 more people were arrested after refusing to drink water blessed by a Buddhist priest. As prosecutors widened their inquiries, those in other areas fell under suspicion. In Goto, as we have seen, there were widespread persecutions, and in nearby Omura a further 110 Christians were seized and kept in such severe conditions that 60 of them died of exposure.

When news of all this reached Western powers, they were outraged. France was particularly vocal as protector of Catholics in non-Catholic countries. For its part, the shogunate might have been willing to compromise (it had abandoned the *fumie* in 1857), but it was not strong enough to resist the powerful anti-foreigner lobby. Any concession to the Great Powers would open them to accusations of weakness, for "*Sonno joi*" was the slogan of the day: Respect the Emperor, Expel the Barbarians!

The fall of the shogunate in 1867 paved the way for an emperor-centered government whose ideology was based on a Shintoist patriotism. Instead of this ushering in a more open age, anti-Christian feeling hardened and signboards were put up warning people against the "abominable religion," for the possibility of Japanese Christians operating as a fifth column worried the new regime just as much as it had the old. In an 1869 exchange, the French foreign minister threatened naval intervention if the mistreatment of Catholics continued. "Your threat shows the good reason we have to fear Christianity, for as soon as trouble arises, there is talk of gunboats," responded the Japanese foreign minister.

One of the most influential figures in the new order, Kido Junichiro, urged action against the Urakami villagers, placing blame firmly on the foreign priests for stirring up trouble and teaching citizens to break the law. In January 1870 a mass deportation took place, in which 3,460 villagers were sent into exile in twenty different domains. Their treatment varied by area, depending on the whim of the authorities. Buddhist and Shinto priests were used to urge the prisoners to convert, while those who resisted were subject to threats and punishment. Rations were limited, there was no winter kimono to withstand the bitter cold, and there were numerous reports of mistreatment. In one case people were made to stand naked in freezing water. So harsh were the conditions that almost a fifth of the exiles died in captivity.

It was at this point that the Urakami villagers unwittingly became a focus of international politics. The new government regarded the treaties with the Great Powers as unfair, but in discussions to get them amended they were told that as long as they persecuted Christians they could hardly be considered civilized— or equal. It was partly to address the issue that the government dispatched the Iwakura Mission (1871–73) on a round-the-world trip. It was a huge and costly undertaking, with a plenipotentiary ambassador accompanied by four vice-ambassadors (three of whom were government ministers) and an entourage of 48 officials and 60 students. The remit included gathering information about the West, and after 260 years of isolation it was hardly surprising that there should be surprises. One was bewilderment at the hold Christianity had on technologically advanced societies, for it seemed to mission members a fairy-tale religion whose holiest book told of voices coming out of the sky. Most baffling of all was that it centered on an executed criminal:

> In every municipality in Europe and America, we find pictures of the dead prisoner, blood-stains all over him, being lowered off the cross. These are hung on hall-walls and house niches and give people the sensation of passing a graveyard, or looking at an execution ground. If this isn't eerie, what in the world is? Yet the Occidentals find it eerie that the East does not have such pictures.

As the mission made its way across America to Europe, it found itself confronted by opposition to Japan's treatment of Christians, particularly in Catholic countries. In Belgium there was even an anti-Japanese demonstration. Realizing that persecution was hindering their objectives, the government decided to quietly change tack. In 1873 the signboards forbidding Christianity were taken down, and de facto toleration was signaled shortly afterwards by release of the exiled villagers. The same year saw adoption of the Gregorian calendar, which measured time from the birth of Christ rather than ascension of the emperor. If Japan couldn't beat the West, it would join them. The Hidden Christians had helped set the country's new agenda.

Refuseniks

In the years that followed, it became apparent that there were an astonishing 50,000 to 60,000 Hidden Christians in all. Catholics were delighted: it not only proved the power of the faith but provided ready-made recruits for the fledgling Church. What could be more natural than having been cut off from the religion for over two hundred years, the believers would line up to rejoin. The process had begun as early as 1866, when three Urakami villagers had taken Mass with Father Petitjean despite the risk of capital punishment. Five years later, even as those arrested in the roundups were being shipped off to exile, Petitjean was smuggling youths to Shanghai to have them trained as priests.

By 1892 the Church was able to announce that about half of the Hidden Christians had become Catholics. It was treated as a source of satisfaction, but why only half? This was twenty years after toleration: why hadn't all of the Hidden Christians rejoined Catholicism? Surely it was for that very reason that they had handed down their faith! Things were not quite that simple, however. For a start, the fourth persecution had reinforced the virtues of secrecy. The policy had served their ancestors well, and many saw no need to change. Besides, rejoining the Church meant accepting that what they practiced was wrong. And if it was wrong, it meant that what their parents had taught them was wrong, as in turn their parents before them. It meant, in short, accepting that their ancestors were condemned to damnation.

Prominent among those who refused to rejoin the Catholic Church were Hidden Christian officeholders, who stood to lose their standing. They had invested too much to give it up easily. Since they were influential figures, their decision affected the choice of ordinary members, who were forced to choose between a baptiser they knew and one they didn't. Group solidarity was clearly a factor in this, as was loyalty to past generations. The attitude of the Church did not help either—the insistence that *kamidana* (Shinto spirit shelf) and *butsudan* (Buddhist altar) be destroyed, for example. Some of the missionaries viewed those who refused to change their way as stubborn heretics. It was a pity, said one, that they were so close to heaven yet destined for hell.

In the end about 30,000 of the "old believers" declined to continue with the practices that had been handed down to them. Already by the 1880s it was clear there was a genuine split, and that what the Hidden Christians were practicing was not so much a distorted form of Catholicism as a religion of their own. To Catholics they were Hanare Kirishitan, or "Separated Christians," and Endo Shusaku told of an encounter that had occurred between them and a French priest. "You are reformed, but we are the original," said an old man to the missionary. The Frenchman responded that he was just the same as the *bateren* who had converted their ancestors but was told that he didn't even look like them. So he went away and returned dressed in the habit of seventeenth-century missionaries. It made little difference. The villagers insisted they were following ways handed down by their ancestors, while modern Catholics had changed. They had a point: the practices had evolved after 1614, and their paths had diverged.

Ground Zero

Following their return from exile, the Urakami Catholics were determined to establish a church worthy of their community. The site they chose could hardly have been more symbolic, for it was that of the magistrate's office where once they had been made to perform the *fumie* ritual of trampling on the icon. Land that had been a curse to them was to be transformed into one of blessing. Construction started in 1895, but lack of funds meant progress relied on voluntary labor, and it was not until 1914 that the church opened. Even then the bell towers were left uncompleted until 1925. With its Romanesque style, some thought it the finest church in East Asia: from a valley of Hidden Christians, Urakami had become a showpiece for Japanese Catholicism.

In 1945 the district once again captured world attention, for on August 9 of that year an atom bomb named Fatman, bigger than that of Hiroshima, laid waste the entire district. Buildings exploded, glass melted and humans fried in one devastating flash. As the mushroom cloud rose, it became apparent that everything and everyone within 1.2 miles of the epicenter had been destroyed. Estimates put the number of dead at around 70,000, with something like the same number suffering radiation illness of varying degrees. Where once people lived and breathed, rocks carried ghostly shadows. Kimono patterns were imprinted on women's flesh.

Nagasaki had not in fact been the primary target; it had been Kokura, which housed a major arsenal. Cloud cover prevented the bombing, and so the planes moved on to their secondary target with the twin towers of the cathedral serving as a directional marker. The bomb exploded in the air halfway between the Mitsubishi Steel Works and the Urakami Ordinance Works. It was just 500 yards from the cathedral, in which a service was in progress with two priests and thirty believers. The building was devastated, as was the entire community. Of the 12,000 Catholics in Urakami, over three-quarters died as a result of the bomb. In a single flash the Truman administration had killed more Christians than in the whole history of Japanese persecution.

How does one balance the dropping of a bomb against the killing of individuals? It's an impossible question to address, for any kind of statement will incur charges of insensitivity. Nonetheless, it's a question any responsible citizen surely has to consider at a time when bombings are being carried out in the name of Western democracy by distant drones in Middle Eastern countries. We prosecute people for torture at Abu Ghraib, but air raids that result in the mass death of innocent citizens are written off as accidents of war.

Although I'd come to Urakami to track down Hidden Christians, I was confronted all around by the effects of the bomb. Remnants of a cathedral wall that survived the blast have been placed in a small park that marks the epicenter, as a grim memorial. Alongside it runs a stream that was once clogged with charred bodies, many of whom had come groping for a drink of water. As I stood in the park, there came the awful realization of life continuing regardless, for all around was the bustling rush of a thriving modern city. People walk their dogs, or saunter around with the vague curiosity of tourists on a day out. The unsettling nature was well captured by W. H. Auden in his poem "Musée des Beaux Arts," where he writes of death taking place even as people go about their daily business.

Around a corner from the park, in a deserted side street, I was shown a simple signboard that stood by the side of a small stone embankment. It marks the miraculous escape of the area's sole survivor, a seven-year-old girl who was playing by herself when she heard the air-raid siren. As she made towards an opening in the embankment that served as makeshift shelter, the force of the blast hurled her against the back and saved her from incineration. Such is the randomness of life. And of death. Shy of publicity, she lives now incognito in another part of Japan. What images haunt her mind in the deep hours of the night, one wonders?

A rebuilt Urakami Cathedral once again dominates the area. The city council wanted to leave the ruins as a memorial, but local Catholics were determined to rebuild it on the same site. It stands as testimony to the strength of the human spirit even in the face of the worst imaginable kind of adversity. On the grounds are displayed remains of the original building, while inside are arranged the heads of corpseless statues in a macabre pile. A helpful nun in the cathedral bookshop told me how she'd come to Nagasaki to help the *hibakusha* (nuclear bomb survivors). It was a generous gesture, for many of those with radiation illness were shunned in the postwar period, particularly when it came to marriage partners. With a glint in her eye, she offered to show me a survivor of the atom bomb, then led me into the church to see a statue known as Hibaku Maria. The ashen color, the charred visage and empty black sockets serve as a ghastly reminder of the apocalyptic moment.

Not far from the cathedral stands Nyokodo, former home of Dr. Nagai Takashi (1908–51), who had ironically already contracted leukemia before the bomb dropped, due to exposure to radiation at work. "For me, the injury to the right side of my body and acute disease caused by the atomic bomb were added to my chronic radiation illness," he wrote. Even so he worked tirelessly on behalf of those suffering in the wake of the bomb. He wrote fondly of life in Urakami, and in books like *A Bell at Nagasaki* (1946) and *Leaving These Children Behind* (1948) he described his affinity with the inhabitants. "The people of Urakami love others as they love themselves, truly a blessing for a person far from home and weary of the hardships of war. That is why I called this house Nyokodo (As Yourself Hermitage) and why I constantly offer prayers of thanks."

Dr. Nagai's house stands on the site where the area's *chokata*, or Hidden Christian leader, lived in Edo times. The doctor had married into the family after boarding with them as a student at Nagasaki Medical College. For seven generations the family had served as the focus of Hidden Christian activities in Urakami, with each succeeding eldest son taking over the duties of the father. The seventh in line, Maogemon Yoshizo, was arrested and killed in 1856—a mere decade before the arrival of Petitjean. The family converted to Catholicism in early Meiji times, and it was Yoshizo's granddaughter whom Dr. Nagai had married.

Nyokodo's history typified the move to Catholicism that had taken place in much of Urakami after toleration of the religion. The minority who continued to practice as Hidden Christians were decimated by the atomic bomb, and I'd read somewhere that the last practicing descendant had died in 1994. It was the end of a remarkable story. News articles said that to find contemporary Hidden Christians, one had to go to the north of the prefecture, to a small island called Ikitsuki off the coast of Hirado. Even then an expert on the subject had told me not to expect too much: "They're more of a museum piece than real practitioners," he suggested. Nevertheless I was anxious to see for myself and set off in the hope of bringing up to date an account that had begun centuries before at the other end of Kyushu. It was to be the last leg of my journey. Would it, I wondered, end with revelations?

Chapter Twelve

Last Rites
(Hirado)

The Protestant connection

Not many foreigners make it to Hirado. It's a pity. The island may be off the beaten track, tucked as it is in the northwestern corner of Kyushu, but there is much to commend it. The physical aspect, for instance. With a population of 25,000, the main town has an intimate but distinctive character, being set around a small bay dominated by a hilltop castle, which at night when it's lit up has a fairy-tale quality. There's historical interest too, for proximity to the continent meant that it played an important role in the comings and goings of ancient times. In the twelfth century Eisai returned here from studying Zen in China and planted the first tea in Japan. In 1550 the Japanese had their first experience of bread, thanks to the Portuguese, who later also introduced tobacco. Beer arrived with the English in 1613.

Historically, Hirado is best known for hosting the Dutch and English "factories" (trading stations). It brings to mind William Adams (1564–1620), the figure fictionalized in James Clavell's *Shogun*. Known in Japan as Miura Anjin, he was not only the first Englishman to visit the country but the only white man ever to be made a samurai. A simple son of Kent, the ship's pilot had arrived in 1600 on a battered Dutch ship after twenty months at sea. Of the original hundred-man crew, only twenty-six remained and eight of those were at death's door. Things were bad but were about to get worse, for the Jesuits in Bungo where the ship landed urged the daimyo to have the Protestant new-comers executed as pirates. They were sent instead to the prison at Osaka Castle, where Adams was interviewed by the country's strongman, Tokugawa Ieyasu:

> Coming before the king, he viewed me well, and seemed to be wonderfully favorable. He made many signs unto me, some of which I understood, and some I did not. In the end, there came one that could speak Portuguese. By him, the king demanded of me, of what land I was, and what moved us to come to his land, being so far off. I showed unto him the name of our country, and that our land had long sought out the East Indies, and desired friendship with all kinds and potentates in way of merchandise, having in our land diverse commodities, which these lands had not. . . . Then he asked whether our country had wars? I answered him yea, with the Spaniards and Portugals, being in peace with all other nations.

From such inauspicious beginnings, Adams pioneered his way through a maze of unknown customs to become a trusted advisor of Ieyasu, for whom he built and captained ships. In his early years he yearned to go back home to his English wife and children, but later when he was offered the chance he passed it up. By that time he was a well-appointed bigamist, with a Japanese wife and an estate of some ninety households at Hemi on the Miura Peninsula near Edo. He held the title of *hatamoto*, which meant he was a direct retainer of the shogun with access

to the court. In addition to his Japanese family he had a mistress
and child at Hirado, where he often came to work for the English factory. It was here too that he died at the age of fifty-five.

Brusque and aloof, Adams was not always easy to get on
with: his fellow countrymen were disconcerted to find he was
as likely to side with the Dutch or Japanese as with themselves.
To their eyes he'd gone native: after becoming a samurai he took
to wearing Japanese clothing, had a pair of swords, and used
the Japanese calendar in his diary. He had a high regard for the
people ("curteous above measure"), but found them "very su-
perstitious in their religion." Though he stuck to his Protestant
beliefs, he registered with the Buddhist temple next to his estate
and even carried a small bronze Buddha with him on his travels.
He'd become a hidden Christian!

During my early years in Japan, when I was on a wild roller-
coaster ride of culture shock, I looked to Adams as a *senpai* (predecessor) who had overcome situations far more extreme than
anything I had to face. Accordingly, I made his monument my
first priority. It's thought his remains would have been laid in the
English graveyard above the town, but the whereabouts were lost
in the destruction of Christian graves in Edo times. Instead three
monuments were put up in 1954 in a hillside park: one has the
names of the eighteen English sailors who died at Hirado; one
says, duplicitously, GRAVE OF MIURA ANJIN; and the third written
in English says IN MEMORY OF WILLIAM ADAMS AND HIS WIFE
MARY HYN. It's as if in death the naturalized samurai had reverted
to being a married Englishman.

His was an extraordinary life by any standards. Born in the
same year as William Shakespeare, he'd been apprenticed to a
London shipyard at age twelve and may well have seen the play-
wright's early plays at the nearby Globe. As a young man he captained a supply ship under Francis Drake in the defeat of the
Spanish Armada and went in search of the Northeast Passage. It

was only at the age of thirty-four that he joined a group of five Dutch ships headed for the Far East, and in Japan he played a crucial part in the country's "Christian century" by conspiring against the Jesuits. From the outset, he and the Dutch were anxious to distance themselves from the Catholics, though it took a lot of persuasion. Matters were not helped when it was discovered that a letter from James I was signed "Defender of the faith," a phrase also used by the Jesuits.

When the missionaries saw the favor Adams enjoyed with Ieyasu, they changed tack and offered him safe passage back to Europe in an attempt to get rid of him. They even tried to convert him. Finally, in what must have been a humiliating move, they asked him to intercede on their behalf: "My former enemies did wonder and at this time must entreat me to doe them a friendship," he noted with satisfaction. Generously, he decided to do "good for evill" and help them out. Meanwhile, however, he continued to tell Ieyasu they wanted to colonize the country.

In 1613 Adams helped set up the English factory, which was located along the harbor from the larger Dutch factory. The arrangement was fine when the two nations were cooperating, but unpleasantly close when relations between them turned nasty. I wandered down to have a look at the stone marker for the English station, then made my way to where reconstruction was in progress on the splendid Dutch building. It was conveniently located by the wharf at the mouth of the harbor, so that boats could ferry goods from the ocean-going vessels anchored offshore. The English proved much less successful than the Dutch, partly because of incompetence and partly because of profligate womanizing. Captain John Saris, who set up the trading station, was a keen collector of erotica and on one occasion was showing a group of well-born women around his cabin when an unexpected occurrence took place, for "the picture of Venus with her sonne Cupid, did hang wantonly set out in a large frame. They, thinking it to be our ladie and her sonne, fell downe and worshipped it, with shewes of great devotion, telling me in a whispering manner that they were Christianos."

The whispering was because Christianity was in disfavor: how did the English traders feel, one wonders, about the persecution? With a mixture of *Schadenfreude* and apprehension, it seems. They were pleased to find the Catholics tormented, but concerned lest the trouble engulf them. When a Franciscan missionary turned up distraught on their doorstep following the fall of Osaka Castle in 1615, the head of the factory, Richard Cocks, was sufficiently moved to give him some silver plate to get to Nagasaki. "I do not rejoice herein," he wrote about the destruction of churches there, while at the same time noting that he was pleased he would no longer have to endure the jibes of Jesuits, for "one could not passe the streets without being by them called *Lutranos* [Lutherans] or *herejos* [heretics]."

The English pulled out in 1623, but the Dutch carried on trading even as the Tokugawa moved towards isolationism. Not only were all foreign Catholics expelled, but in 1639 the shogunate even ordered half-blood children and their mothers out of the country. The Dutch were charged with transferring them to their base in Batavia (Java), and the small Hirado History Museum proudly displays one of the four letters to survive that were smuggled back to friends and relatives. With the expulsion of the Portuguese from Dejima, the Tokugawa sought an excuse to corral the Dutch there in order to take over the lucrative trade benefits. They found a pretext in two new buildings put up by the Dutch in Hirado, above the doors of which was written the year of completion. Since this was according to the Christian calendar, it was technically in breach of the strict laws against the religion. With that, Hirado's foreign connections were cut, and all that remained were pockets of Hidden Christians. But how come they were there in the first place?

The Catholic connection

Following my homage to William Adams, I made my way up the other side of the bay where I was to visit Urabe Tomoyuki at the castle museum. The eighteenth-century buildings, rebuilt after the war, offer a panorama of harbor and open sea. On a clear day it's said you can see the island of Iki, one of the stepping-stones on the way to Korea. Down below, the elegant Western-style buildings of the Dutch factory stand out just as prominently as they would have done four hundred years earlier.

"Christianity in Hirado began with Francis Xavier," said Urabe-san. "He came here three times. The first time was in June 1550 to pick up post from a Portuguese ship. A few months later he came again on his way to Miyako [Kyoto]. The daimyo, Matsuura Takanoba, wanted good relations with the Portuguese, so Xavier was allowed to preach, and in twenty days he had more success than in his year in Kagoshima. In Miyako he was refused an audience with the emperor, so he returned here again for a third time to pick up gifts and robes for his meeting with the daimyo of Yamaguchi."

Hirado had served the missionary well, and the connection is cherished in the striking Francis Xavier Memorial Church built in 1931, the Gothic steeple of which pierces the roofscape of the town's temple district. In 2006, to celebrate the five hundredth anniversary of Xavier's birth, a direct descendant of the family arrived from Macao—on a water scooter. It was the smallest vessel in maritime history to cross from southern China to Japan. The missionary himself had suffered badly from seasickness on his voyage. What would he have made of his descendant, one wonders?

"By 1555 there were about five hundred Christians in the Hirado area," continued Urabe. "Takanoba gave land to them for a cemetery and erected a crucifix. There's no doubt that his intention was to get guns, cannon and other weapons. He even said he would convert himself, but instead pressed two of his relatives to do so."

In the areas under control of the two converts, missionaries were able to make inroads, and in 1555 Father Gaga, a Portuguese priest, belied his name by holding elaborate funeral services that attracted wide attention. He also used loan words instead of Japanese terms for Christian concepts, which led some believers to give up the religion because they realized for the first time that it wasn't actually Buddhism. Nonetheless, in 1558 the first mass conversion in Japan took place on Ikitsuki, and in 1561 the whole island of Takushima was baptised and became the first fully Catholic community in the country.

Friction soon developed, however. The missionary Gaspar Vilela was expelled from the domain "because of his passionate and eager missionary work," as Urabe put it—a diplomatic way of saying that he burned Buddhist idols. Then Portuguese and Hirado merchants came to blows in a dispute over prices, leading to deaths on either side. The daimyo tried to win back favor by giving permission for the Church of the Pregnant Santa Maria, which became a regional base for the mission. Children were taught prayers and songs in Latin, some of which were transmitted orally to modern times by local Hidden Christians.

"Because the priests felt difficulties in dealing with a non-Christian lord," continued Urabe, "they advised Portuguese ships to use the harbor of Lord Omura, who was a Christian, rather than Hirado. Takanobu was furious and attacked a Portuguese ship in revenge. From then on, the treatment of Christians became very strict. His son, Matsuura Shigenobu, was even more hostile, because he resented the way missionaries treated his father."

Persecution started relatively early in the domain. In 1592 Shigenobu not only ordered the expulsion of missionaries from Hirado but started to suppress Japanese converts. Following

Hideyoshi's crucifixion of the 26 Martyrs in 1597, he introduced more severe measures. Two years later came a decisive development, when the domain's leading Christians, the Koteda family, were expelled to Nagasaki for refusing to attend the Buddhist funeral of the former daimyo. With them went some six hundred fellow believers. It tore the heart out of the Christian community, though those who remained continued to cling to their faith in secret.

In 1620, at risk to his life, Christovao Ferreira sneaked into the territory and heard 1,300 confessions; it was work such as this that led to his appointment as head of the Japan mission. Other missionaries secretly entered from Macao, one of whom was an Italian named Camillo Constanzo. He had first come to Japan in 1605, before being expelled to Macao in 1614. Following his return seven years later, he was caught and burned to death on Tabira beach facing towards Hirado. Hundreds gathered for the event, and it was said that he continued singing *Laudate Dominum* and crying "Holy! Holy!" even after he was engulfed in flames and black smoke. (The site is marked now by a monument, which overlooks Hirado Sound.)

There were Japanese martyrs too in these years, and as is usual in persecutions, the authorities sought out leaders and their families in order to cow others into submission. As prosecutors saw the effect of martyrs' relics on believers, they were concerned to ensure there were no remains. There were reports of people being thrown off cliffs, and of children tied up together in straw jackets to be tossed into the sea. For the most part, though, the persecution was sporadic rather than thoroughgoing.

"In 1639," said Urabe, "a crucial event for the future of Christians in Hirado happened. Mondo Ukibashi, a retainer of the daimyo, betrayed the clan and informed the shogunate that Hirado was Christian. It was a great shock, and to prove his loyalty to the shogun the daimyo started a wave of executions, the last of which took place in 1645. After that he was able to report that Christianity had been eradicated."

Thereafter Hirado fell into line with the rest of the country. As elsewhere, a system of controls and checks was put in place—citizens had to register with Buddhist temples; a Religious Prosecution Office was set up; and *fumie* were specially brought from Nagasaki. On the surface all was compliance and conformism, but beneath the surface, in true Japanese style, there was more than met the eye.

Museum piece

In recent years the little island of Ikitsuki has created big interest. Five miles long and nearly two at its widest point, the island hosts the last major Hidden Christian community. Of its 7,300 inhabitants, up to 1,000 honor the once forbidden faith of their ancestors, and they have attracted much attention from the outside world. "Japan's crypto-Christians," ran a *Time* magazine article. "Once banned Christianity withers in an old stronghold," proclaimed the *New York Times*. "Japan's Hidden Christians face extinction," echoed Reuters. "Today's Hidden Christians are now under threat more than ever before," announced Australian radio. The consensus, quite clearly, is that even on Ikitsuki the Hidden Christians are dying out.

The island lies across a continuous truss bridge from Hirado, which at 1,312 feet is the longest of its type in the world. Before it was built in 1991, access was by boat, and I was told that at one time relations between Catholics and Hidden Christians had been so bad that people would be refused passage if they were from the wrong side of the divide. Now it's a simple matter of driving twenty minutes from Hirado, and I took a rental car across the bridge, where I found the island museum, conveniently, to be the first stop on the island. Its curator, ethnologist

Nakazono Shigeo, is the first stop for researchers too, for though the island's Hidden Christians are more open than in Goto and Sotome, they still need shielding from intrusive outsiders. Given the demands on his time, I was lucky to get a personal tour of the museum.

"Hidden Christians can be divided into two types," Nakazono said. "In the southern group—Sotome, Goto and Urakami—they were based on Bastian's calendar and annual observances. Here and in Hirado they were based on 'closet gods'—in Japanese we say *nandogami* or *gozensama*. They include sacred objects such as images and ritual items. You can see the 'closet worship' here. It's typical for Ikitsuki."

We were on the second floor of the museum (the first is given over to the island's former whaling industry), and before us was a *nando*—a small back room for storage space. The exhibit showed how it was converted by Hidden Christians into a shrine, resembling a large tokonoma alcove. At the back was a hanging scroll of a Japanese woman in an opened kimono with baby at her breast—a well-disguised image of the Madonna. Beneath on a trunk were laid out some of the "closet gods": a ceramic vase filled with holy water, a rope scourge, and a Maria Kannon statue. On the floor a single cushion indicated where the worshipper would have kneeled.

Next to the closet was a simple small room where gatherings took place. Over the wooden floor matting was laid, and signs had been put to indicate where officials would have sat. (This being Japan there was a ranking system.) From a wall-mounted speaker came recordings of the *orashio* prayers they would have recited. When Professor Tagita Koyo studied them in the 1920s, he was told the words were deliberately meaningless in order to confuse outsiders. Later, however, he came to realize they were pigeon Latin: "Deo gratis, Amen" had become "biya garassa, ammeizus."

"Each region, like Sotome, Urakami and Hirado, had its own kind of organization," continued Nakazono. "There's a researcher in Tokyo working on whether they were related to differences between Jesuits, Franciscans and Dominicans. Here in Ikitsuki there were seven Hidden Christian areas, which formed into subdivisions. They centered around gatherings called *tsumoto,* which were put on by groups of households. In some areas the *tsumoto* rotated from house to house, but in others the place was fixed. Baptism was the most important ritual, and in this picture you can see them collecting baptism water from Nakae Island, which is uninhabited."

In the photograph, four men in blue kimono knelt reverentially before a crack in a rock face, at the base of which were set candles. Small containers stood nearby.

"They collect the water that comes out. It's considered sacred because the island was a place of martyrdom in 1622 and 1624, when fourteen people or more were executed there. The baptism water is called San Juan-sama because two of the people executed on the island were called Juan or Johannes. Maybe too because of John the Baptist. The water was very special for the Hidden. They put it in these ceramic containers," he pointed to some open-mouthed bottles from the mouths of which protruded sticks used for sprinkling water during rituals. "Recently they use plastic bottles because they don't break so easily," he said with a smile. "And here you can see a baptism."

The picture showed an ordinary living room, crammed full with furniture and decorations, with three children kneeling before a man in a blue kimono, applying water to their foreheads with the stick from the ceramic container. It was a curiously relaxed affair: the children wore everyday clothing, the room was cluttered, and the only indication that it was a special occasion was a collection of congratulatory saké bottles. In case of emergency, the whole event could be easily disguised as a party. (The carousing apparently continues all night, so those saké bottles were not for show!)

A large proportion of the "closet gods" are representational in nature, reflecting the importance of visual aids for the early mission, which had to work with peasants who were largely illiterate. Medals, statues and paintings were shipped over in bulk from Europe, and in 1561 Luis de Almedia noted a Portuguese ship unloading a huge cargo of such items at Ikitsuki. For Hidden Christians they were imbued with a sacred awe, as if to compensate for the lack of doctrine and Church rites. Rather than representing the divine, they simply *were* divine. It was as if what they represented no longer mattered: they were sacred in themselves, much like the *goshintai* (sacred body) of Shinto shrines that house the spirit of the *kami*.

We turned next to a collection of paintings that looked at first sight like children's efforts. The Jesuits had not only brought over works of art from Europe, but had set up a school to train native artists. Over time, many of the originals were lost, damaged or destroyed: replacements were painted by amateurs, from memory or imagination. Whether deliberate or not, they were sometimes difficult to recognize as Christian. One showed Joseph and Mary with Japanese features, another had the baby Jesus looking much like a monkey, and a third showed Saint Sebastian in seventeenth-century Portuguese clothing. John the Baptist had a *chomage* hairstyle, like a samurai. In an interesting take on the Trinity, a demonic God with Daruma-like features hovered over an Asiatic couple representing Jesus and Mary.

"Do you recognize this?" Nakazono asked, pointing to a scourge. "It was not used like Catholics do for flagellation, but for purification like this," he said, making the sweeping gesture done by shrine priests when purifying worshippers. It brought to mind the incident with Francis Xavier in Kagoshima, when he was asked to provide a healing technique for believers (in accord with the Japanese tendency to seek worldly benefit from religion). In response, he had suggested lightly hitting the patient with a scourge over the place affected. The Roman Catholic technique had been adapted by Hidden Christians to deal with impurities in houses as well as people. Made of hemp rope, the scourge had been turned into a spiritual tool in the Japanese tradition.

The next exhibit showed tiny paper crosses, which as "closet gods" had one big advantage: they could be swallowed in case of emergency! They served a variety of uses, being slipped into kimono sleeves like lucky charms, or under the kimonos of corpses as a safeguard before Buddhist funerals. They were also stuck in bamboo poles at the sides of fields as an aid to fertility. I was struck by their use in purification rituals, for following the waving of the scourge, the paper crosses were apparently used to seal the area. Anyone familiar with Wicca paganism will recognize the technique, for witches too are concerned to seal their sacred circle. The Hidden Christians were using magic! Farmers and fishermen are close to the elemental world, and it was somehow fitting that they should have brought out the pagan roots of the religion.

"These *ofuda* are unique to the Hirado area," said Nakazono, indicating some wooden pieces. "They were used for divination purposes. There were sixteen in all: one for each of the fifteen stages of the cross, plus an extra one on which was written 'Amen.' They were divided into three groups representing the division of the rosary: Sorrow, Joy and Glory. On the first Sunday of the month representatives would meet and pick one of the *ofuda,* which would foretell the fortune of their households."

It reminded me of the picking of *omikuji* fortune slips at Shinto shrines. Anyone who has lived in Japan knows of the country's fascination with fortune telling, which can be traced back to ancient divination practices using tortoiseshell and deer antlers. Here was a Hidden Christian gloss on the tradition.

Before taking leave of the museum, I asked Nakazono about present-day activities. Most took place around the New Year period, he told me. Christmas is held before the winter solstice and celebrated by Hidden Christians in their own way. At New Year it was customary to visit the *tsumoto* meeting place, and over the next few days officials did the rounds of houses to purify them for the coming year. On January 16 there was a public ceremony at a martyrs site called Danjiku, where *orashio* prayers are said in honor of those who died. And how about the current state of affairs, I wanted to know?

"Now, there's a big difference from before," he said. "Now they are more conscious of being part of a tradition that is dying out. So they want to preserve it, not just to continue the faith of their parents. But the number is going down all the time. In recent years two more groups disbanded. Fifteen years ago there were twenty-one groups, now there are just four."

He took me into his office to show me an article in the *Asahi Shimbun*, which quoted one of the island's Hidden Christians, Matsuyama Ayuzo. "We inherited this Old Christianity from our ancestors and we wanted it to continue forever," he commented. "It's sad. The tradition of our ancestors is disappearing." Without young believers to succeed the present generation, it seems the religion is poised like an endangered species on the point of extinction. Kirk Sandvig, who has been investigating the contemporary situation, figures that there are fewer than a hundred practitioners in all, most over sixty, and that people are fully resigned to this being the end of the line. The last Hidden Christians are themselves fast becoming a museum piece.

Into the sunset

Following the museum visit I went to have lunch in a sushi shop and fell into conversation with the elderly owner. It was a homely place facing the sea, and he was an affable sort with an inclination for idle chat. He told me he'd grown up in a Hidden Christian family before World War Two and joined a small group at weekends to memorize the *orashio*.

"It was terrible having to learn the prayers. They didn't make sense at all. I had to learn words all in katakana [phonetic script]. Some had no meaning. There was no punctuation: you didn't know where to pause or stop. When I got home I wrote it all down, though you were not supposed to. And you had to sit *seiza* [with folded knees]. Ah, my legs hurt. I got cramp, and in winter it was cold. But when I was nineteen, I left home and made money as a pachinko pro in Imari. Then I met a hostess and got a job in a nightclub. I stayed for thirty years and only came back when I was fifty-five, to start this sushi shop. Now I'm seventy-six. But I'm still *genki* [healthy]," he said with a laugh.

I noticed on the wall, among the sumo autographs, that there were the Seven Lucky Gods and other charms from a local shrine, so I asked him if he followed Shinto.

"No, I'm Zen, more or less," he said, "But I don't care about that. Just I pay them every year. And pretty soon they'll bury me. But I'm thinking of changing to Catholic. It's cheaper because they don't make you pay for a *kaimyo* [posthumous name]. I prefer to save my money for women. And drinking. It's my way to paradise," he said with a laugh.

The hedonistic chef exemplified the effects of modernization that had disrupted traditional ways in the twentieth century. Memorization of prayers had little meaning to him: it was a past he was happy to escape. It represented more than an individual loss for the Hidden Christians, for he had been the oldest son in his family, responsible for carrying on the family tradition. It meant a household lost forever to a tradition stretching back over four hundred years.

Afterwards, I drove up to a martyr's monument, past a statue of the bodhisattva Kannon that stands fifty feet high and weighs 150 tons. It's an improbably massive feature for a small island, built to look out compassionately over the sea and the fishermen who risk their lives. My goal by contrast was an enormous cross that commemorates Gaspar Nishi. Christened after the man who baptised him, the samurai had become leader of the island's Christians following the expulsion of the Koteda family in 1599. Ten years later he was arrested and condemned to death. Though he asked to be crucified, the punishment was unknown on the island and he was granted the privilege instead of being beheaded where a large cross had once stood. Afterwards his corpse was used for blade testing and chopped to pieces. His wife and oldest son were also executed and buried on the same hill.

Now the site is once more marked by a large cross, erected in 1992 on a headland looking towards Hirado. A laborer patching up some of the stonework pointed out Nakae Island in the pristine blue sea. "Nearest island to paradise," he said (a reference, I found later, to the last words of a martyred farmer: "Heaven is very close here"). Since it was the island from which Hidden Christians drew their sacred water, it was supposedly off-limits and I wondered if the laborer had been there. "Yes," he answered dismissively, "there's nothing but rocks." Dead spirits and rocks have a long association in Japan, as elsewhere. Stonehenge, the pyramids, the tomb of Jesus—rocks speak to the immortality of the soul, and in their sacred island the Hidden Christians had created their own undying memorial.

Not far from Gaspar Nishi's monument was another martyrs site, Senninzuka, which translates as "Mound of a Thousand People" ("thousand" here signifying a large number), and I was surprised to find it marked by a torii. Imperial mounds are often marked by the Shinto symbol, but it's unexpected—possibly unique—to find one for a Christian burial site. The mound commemorates the mass killing in 1645. Up to that point only leaders had been executed, but the Hirado daimyo ordered an assault on ordinary believers in an attempt to prove his loyalty to the Tokugawa shogunate. In what he hoped would be the final solution, he sent his chief retainer to Ikitsuki to wipe out the religion, and it's said the beach was turned red with blood. Now the victims are honored every year by Hidden Christians, and in a generous interfaith gesture the Shinto priest too prays for the souls of the dead during the annual festival of the local shrine.

Afterwards, I called in at Yamada Church, curious to see a building whose walls are decorated with butterfly wings. Built in 1912, it was said to be a rare example of cooperation between the island's Catholics and Hidden Christians. An earlier priest had been a keen lepidopterist, and the butterfly wings are set in colorful circles against a blue mural. The effect is almost gaudy, complemented with some fine woodwork and red carpeting. In lieu of pews, heated carpets are laid out for worshippers to sit on—a Japanese touch. The homely atmosphere was in contrast with the plain exterior, and as I looked around the outside I found myself gazing at a small rock garden in which stood a Madonna and other figures. Several churches in the region house replica of the Lourdes grotto, complemented with carp in some cases, and I was musing on whether this was linked to the cult of cuteness in Japan when my reverie was interrupted by a nun. I told her of my interest in Hidden Christians, and she responded with some forthright views.

"We can't say they're bad, but they are a kind of new religion like some sects of Buddhism. We should respect them. On the radio recently someone said that they are like Okinawa stew, because they throw in everything—a little bit of Buddhism, a *kamidana*, worship of God as well as *yama no kami* (mountain spirit). I don't like that kind of joke. And I don't like the thinking of Professor Miyazaki, do you know him? He said the Hidden

Christians are afraid of giving up their religion because they would be punished by God for having made a wrong choice. But that's not right. They want to respect their ancestors, that's why they continue their faith.

"Things have changed since the war, you see. Now our relations are friendly. In the 1970s several Hidden Christians joined us, but those who didn't, that was fine. We don't press them to join us now, but if they ask to pray together, of course we do. And sometimes they come to us for baptism water if they can't get their own. In our nursery here we have children from Hidden Christian houses. There are many of them over there," she said, pointing to the nearby village. "But they are becoming fewer. We all are. You know, when I was young there were a hundred seventy children in the elementary school. Now there are just forty-five.

"One of my friends was a Hidden, and he kept a special room for the closet gods. It was on the second floor, very private. No one could sleep there. But now his son put the closet gods next to the tokonoma downstairs where everyone can see them. In other places they would not do like that. You know, when the pope came to Japan, my friend went to see him. For the sake of his ancestors, he said. But when he was in a ship accident, badly burned and dying, he never thought of becoming Catholic. He just kept saying *orashio* prayers like before. Maybe he went to heaven anyway. Some other Hidden Christians, when they are dying, they call the priest and get baptised. So it just depends, you see."

She asked me where else I had been, and I told her of my visits around the region. When I mentioned Sotome, talk turned to Endo Shusaku. "Did you know the Japanese film of *Silence* was shot near here?" she asked. "I was on the ferry coming over to the island once and met the main actress. But still I didn't see the film because the Nagasaki bishop said we shouldn't. I didn't read the book either, and if you ask me I think it would be better if Endo had not written it."

All of a sudden she asked, "Would you like to see where the seminary from Osaka came for seven or eight months? When Hideyoshi banned the Christians, they brought the seminary all the way here to this island. It was here for seven or eight months." She went over to collect her car, then told me to follow her and shot off at terrifying speed along the island lanes. I could barely keep up, and pretty soon she'd disappeared completely up ahead of me. There was something surreal about a tearaway sixty-year-old nun racing along the bendy roads, the stuff of comedy indeed, but I found her eventually waiting for me by the roadside. We walked down a narrow lane to a courtyard in which there was a small hall.

"This is a meeting place for Hidden Christians, and the seminary stood over there," she said pointing to a wooded area. "All the houses around here are Hidden Christian, and maybe that was why they sited the seminary here. It was a remote place, surrounded by Christians, you see. By the way, the people here don't sing aloud when chanting prayers, but those in the next village do. It's interesting isn't it, these small differences."

Before leaving, she gave me directions to Koshiro Hill, another place of martyrdom. Legend has it that a samurai of the Hirado clan had been sent to track down a Christian fugitive, but that during the pursuit he was struck blind. Some unknown strangers helped him, and when he found out they were Christian he converted and was baptised as Pablo. Afterwards his sight was miraculously restored. Later, however, he was arrested and executed, his burial site being revered by Hidden Christians as San Paburo-sama. It consists of a simple tomb-like monument in a small clearing, and it's said that anyone who cuts wood here will become ill.

The villager whom I asked for directions insisted that I remove my shoes before entering the grove—it's sacred ground sanctified by the blood of a martyr. There were offerings of saké as you'd find at a Shinto shrine, a small stone torii, what looked like a Jizo, and a statue of the popular Daikokuten deity. Such was the camouflage I couldn't see anything connected with Christianity at all. During Edo times, that would have been a necessity of course, but how curious that it should continue to be the case nowadays. I took it as symptomatic of the way Japanese cling to tradition, reluctant to make changes unless there's a compelling reason.

From Paburo-sama it was but a short drive to the end of the island and the strangely shaped cliffs that featured in the adaptation of *Silence*. Beyond them, at the northern tip of the island, stands a small lighthouse with a viewing platform over open sea and curving bays. In the afternoon sun, the islands of Hirado were laid out like a painting, with far-off Iki island barely visible on the horizon. A poetic touch was added to the scene by a haiku inscribed on a nearby rock.

> The migrating birds
> With this wandering poet
> On martyrs' island

The drive back took me along the less populated side of the island, with green fields to one side and rocky shoreline on the other. Known as the Sunset Line, the road opens up to the western sea, affording delightful views in the late afternoon. Settlements are few, and the sense of remoteness was emphasized by a road sign warning BEWARE OF COWS. First time I'd seen that in Japan! Down a narrow lane a fork in the road gave onto a cul-de-sac, from the end of which a path led through a wooded area and down a rough stone staircase that dropped steeply towards the sea. DANJIKU, announced the signboard.

In 1645 a family had taken shelter here on the shoreline, hiding from the persecution unleashed on the island. It's thought they were intending to escape to a nearby island such as Goto, but their hideout was discovered when daimyo officials patrolling by boat spotted the family's child, who had wandered out. They were subsequently executed. Now every year in January Hidden Christians hold a ceremony open to the public to commemorate the dead. Fishermen come here too to pray for a good catch and safety at sea. Mindful of the past, they keep a tradition of never arriving by boat.

The hideout lies in a thicket of bamboo and camellia, to which a stone path has been built. Inside, a simple marker announced that it was a historical site, and a few small rocks had been arranged into a makeshift shrine before which were strewn small saké cups. There was a vase with wild flowers, and someone had thought to add an Anpanman doll for the child. It's a peaceful spot, and musing on the past I sat for a while on a nearby rock as the sun slowly set below the horizon. Golden rays spilled downwards to kiss the sparkling sea as distant islands melted into the crimson haze. The undersides of dark clouds were singed orange by the fiery conflagration, and only the chatter of birds disturbed the lulling motion of the sea. It was an idyllic scene, and incongruous as it was I had a feeling of oneness. How odd that here of all places people should have killed each other over a simple difference of belief.

Heritage

Kawakami Shigetsugu is an "open Hidden." His maternal grandfather was a baptiser in the village of Neshiko on the island of Hirado, and he remembers as a child being brought up with Hidden Christian legends about martyrs and faraway lands. Though his mother married into a Buddhist household, as a child he spent a lot of time at the house of his grandparents. Meetings took place in a back room in which they would recite chants with mysterious words. Along with *kamidana* and *butsudan*, the house had a medallion with a cross, a scourge and *ofuda* fortune tablets. At New Year he would play lucky dip with them and press the selected *ofuda* to his head saying "Atosama"—code name for the Christian God.

Now, Kawakami represents Neshiko as a city councilor for Hirado and is anxious to promote the village history. Christianity had arrived in the earliest years of the mission, he told me, and a public cross was erected to mark the community faith. The foreigners had made a strong impression on the villagers.

"The missionaries then were more successful than the contemporary Church," he said. "We should respect them. They had few resources but a lot of dedication. People saw the work they did, so they listened to their message. When they first appeared, they were strange beings with special powers and hidden knowledge. People called them Indians. They spoke of love and equality: can you imagine? To the villagers it was like the smell of fresh air."

The Hidden Christians had survived in Neshiko because the village was isolated and self-sufficient—all farmers and fishermen. Believers ran a secret organization that helped out other members, and marriages were arranged when children were still young, often between cousins. It fostered a tendency towards closedness and secrecy that continued even into modern times.

"Neshiko is different from Ikitsuki," said Kawakami. "We used to work together, but Ikitsuki became open whereas the Kakure here kept their religion secret. It was a kind of 'safety lock,' you see. If the rituals or objects were exposed to outsiders, they might become polluted. Also our traditions are different from Ikitsuki. For example, instead of 'closet gods' we say '*kami* of the cross.'"

We had met at the Hirado Christian Museum, located in Neshiko, from where Kawakami took me on a tour of the village. The population stands at 540, almost a third of what it was in

the 1950s before the economic boom lured the young to big cities like Osaka. Now, as with so many rural places, it was top-
heavy with the elderly. The pride of the village is its beach,
selected by the Ministry of the Environment as one of Japan's
best eighty-eight. Goodness knows how they arrived at the decision, though the sheltered bay and short stretch of white sand are
pleasant enough, but its distinguishing feature is not so much
scenic beauty as its unusual history. In 1635, as many as seventy Christians were put to death here, no doubt in full view of
the villagers. Earlier, around 1563, it had witnessed one of the
very earliest executions when a former Buddhist priest turned
Christian refused to perform an official rite. The place of execution is marked by a rock, known as the Ascension Stone, revered
as the village's most sacred site.

A statue of the Virgin Mary overlooks the beach: "Hidden
Christians loved her deeply because they felt she would forgive
them," said Kawakami. Nearby stands the Hama Hachiman
Shrine, established in the 1630s by the Hidden Christians themselves as "camouflage." Ironically, one of the stone lanterns had
been donated by the domain's prosecutor. In times of persecution, believers had hidden between the rocks behind the shrine,
and looking around at the bay as a whole I couldn't help reflecting that sunbathing on one of Japan's Top 88 Beaches came with
some unsettling associations.

From a sacred rock we walked to a sacred tree. According to
tradition, a mother and child hiding in a nearby field of barley
had been caught and executed beneath the tree, which had absorbed their blood. Legend had it that if you cut a branch it
would bleed, and out of respect the tree was left standing by the
roadside while others were removed. Uncovering some grass at
its base, Kawakami showed me a Jizo statue that had been left by
a farmer who inadvertently damaged the tree while burning off
stubble from his field. His daughter had fallen ill with cancer

shortly afterwards, and fearing it was a curse from the tree he made an offering of the Buddhist statue—an interesting case of interfaith practice.

Afterwards Kawakami took me to Ushiwaki Wood, another site to which a legend attaches. In the time of persecution, a man working for the daimyo came to Neshiko in disguise and took work with a family of six, subsequently marrying one of the daughters. Having taken him into their family, they felt able to disclose to him that they were Christian. The very next morning all six of them were arrested, and after refusing to reveal the names of other Christians, they were executed on the beach. Their burial site, here in the wood, became a place of worship in Edo times, and Kawakami told me that it had been customary on New Year's Day to pay respects under cover of making the first visit of the year (*hatsumode*) to the nearby Shinto shrine.

We entered the small copse and stood in the opening before the grave. Dark crows cawed ominously. "In recent times," Kawakami told me, "a worker was trying to thin the forest when all of a sudden he got a kind of electric shock and had to stop. It was like lightning, he said. He didn't understand what it was, but it made him stop. Since then it has been a custom never to cut any of the wood." Like sacred rocks, trees too have a long association with the spirits of the dead, as if drawing the human essence in through their roots. In reaching up towards heaven, they provide a living bridge between this world and the next. Small wonder that our ancestors saw them as sacred.

The tour of the village, like that of Ikitsuki, had shown how important reverence of martyrs sites was for Hidden Christians. Bereft of church and sacraments, the sites had acted as an important part of the religion, providing a locus for their worship and a common sense of heritage. By cultivating the memory of the victims, the community renewed their resolve and affirmed their ancestors had not died in vain. Moreover, the protective spirit of the martyrs functioned like a Shinto *kami*, or in Buddhist terms as an intermediary between this world and the next in the manner of a bodhisattva. For over two centuries villagers had maintained worship of their martyrs in secret, without arousing the attention of the authorities. It was a remarkable achievement.

Back at the museum, Kawakami took me inside and conversation turned to the relationship with Catholicism. In Meiji times, Kawakami told me, a Catholic priest had come to convert the villagers, but they had refused because they didn't want to throw away three hundred years of tradition. "We're the real Christians," they thought. "We're the ones who were persecuted, endured and survived. Why should we give up?" Before us was a panel that gave three reasons for the continuation of Hidden Christians into the modern age.

1) They consider it right to preserve the tradition of their ancestors.
2) They do not want to give up the Buddhist and Shinto aspects of their faith.
3) They were afraid that to abandon their ancestors would be a sin.

Now, as elsewhere, the Hidden Christians in Neshiko had grown elderly and were diminishing in number. What did Kawakami think about the future? "Sadly, the organization here had to disband in 1992," he told me. "Two hundred households had a meeting and dissolved the organization. There were no longer enough people to perform the ceremonies. Being an official is a lot of work, and there is a lot of memorization. A baptiser like my grandfather had to do austerities before rituals, such as purifying himself with cold water, no meat or sex—even hugging his own child was taboo. Can you imagine? And at New Year officials had to go around purifying thirty houses or more.

Each one took about forty minutes. It was too much. No one was able to do it. People thought that it was necessary to do it properly as taught by our ancestors, or not do it at all. So we disbanded the organization. If people wanted, they could continue on their own."

Now Kawakami is working hard to ensure Neshiko is part of the official application by Churches and Christian Sites in Nagasaki to be a UNESCO World Heritage Site. The application will be formally made in 2013, and he's keen to make sure that Hidden Christians are not obscured by the Catholic Church's ability to display historic buildings and official martyrdom sites. By contrast, Hidden Christians have little in the way of physical property. In response he has organized seminars, and in 2008 summoned a Hidden Christian summit with three hundred participants. He also runs a Martyrs Festival at Neshiko to raise awareness and has been instrumental in getting funding for excavation of the small sixteenth-century church that once stood on a hill overlooking the beach. His efforts may lead to greater recognition of the Hidden Christians, ironically just at a time when they seem to be passing out of existence.

Looking at the decline of Hidden Christians, Stephen Turnbull in his study of Ikitsuki identified a number of contributing factors, chief among which are social mobility and modern communications. A faith that was able to preserve itself under persecution has sadly withered in an age of openness, for contemporary lifestyles clash with practices that were forged in the closed communities of a former time. Arranged marriage within a narrow circle of believers has given way to freedom of choice. Schools are now often removed from their community, exposing children to outside ideas. Sons are unwilling to sacrifice their free time for a practice that makes no sense to them, and women are unwilling to do the lengthy preparations that the male-dominated rituals demand. A once proud tradition has run out of time.

Cultural roots

So what had my journey taught me on the broad sweep through 460 years of history? One thing was clear: the Hidden Christians were neither as hidden nor as Christian as their name suggests. The faith had undergone many changes during the long years of persecution, as a result of which it had diverged so far from the original that it was often unrecognizable. In acknowledgment of this, some contemporary practitioners refer to themselves simply as Hidden (*Kakure*), dropping the Christian part. Interestingly, when groups disband the members don't necessarily revert to Catholicism, but instead join Buddhist temples or turn to Shinto. "Kakure Kirishitan should be regarded as another form or expression of Japanese folk religion," writes professor Miyazaki. Believers had paradoxically come to adopt the very traits that their ancestors had risked their lives to reject!

The developments bear out the effect of Endo's "mudswamp." Its constituent elements can be described as polytheistic, syncretic and this-worldly, rooted in reverence for ancestors and emphasizing ritual over doctrine. As such, it's at odds with a monotheistic dogma like Christianity. It helps explain one of the great mysteries about Japan: how, after 150 years of fervid Westernization, the percentage of Christians remains at something like 1 percent. It's staggeringly low, considering the huge amount of money and personnel poured in by Western churches. "Few countries on the face of the earth are more resistant to and more difficult for Christian mission endeavors. It even exceeds Islamic resistance," said Lawrence Spalink in 2007, field director of the Christian Reformed World Missions, who noted there were more church members in Iraq than in Japan.

Yet though Japanese have resisted Christianity, they are infatuated with Western ways—even with Christian ways. It's common, for example, to celebrate Christmas; 70 percent of weddings are Christian-style; and many of the nation's educational institutions are Christian. How can one explain it? It seems that despite the fascination there is a deep-rooted conflict between professing belief in Christianity and something one can only refer to as "Japaneseness." The feeling is captured in Endo's *Deep River,* where Mitsuko says to her friend, Otsu: "You're a strange man. You're Japanese, aren't you? It makes my teeth stand on edge just to think of you as a Japanese believing in the European Christianity nonsense." The reaction may be extreme, but it's not untypical, because there's a fundamental difference in worldview: Christians look to the truth, but Japanese to truths. How interesting then that there is no distinction between singular and plural in the Japanese language.

As my journey was nearing its end, I happened to talk to a Japanese woman who told me she prayed every evening before she went to bed to *kamisama* (a respectful name for god). Which *kamisama*, I asked, in the analytical manner that characterizes Westerners. "The *kamisama* in heaven," she answered as if it was self-evident. But what heaven? I persisted, bluntly. Only when pressed did she even consider the matter. Her *kamisama*, it turned out, was a nameless composite embracing Jesus, all the buddhas and the whole multitude of Shinto *kami*. It was one in all, and all in one. No singular, no plural.

The underlying unity of "the masks of God" were detailed most famously by Joseph Campbell, who in an interview with Bill Moyers said that "Every god, every religion, every mythology is true in this sense. It is true as metaphorical of the human and cosmic mystery." The Japanese long ago realized that the divine comes in multiple guises, and in consequence developed a natural inclination to syncretism. It is exemplified by the Hidden Christians of Hirado, who not only kept their closet gods but maintained a *kamidana* (*kami* shelf), *butsudan* (Buddhist altar) and worship of house spirits. In reverting to a combinatory belief, they were reverting to cultural type.

The worldview was formed in ancient times by customs and practices that have since come to be called Shinto, and I'd reached the conclusion that here lies the key to an understanding of Japanese culture. Not in Zen, as D. T. Suzuki had it, but Shinto. A Hidden Christian woman whom Christal Whelan interviewed in her research on Goto illustrates the point. In an attempt to convert her, a Catholic priest had been giving her Bible lessons. "What a strange book," she said, "I understood nothing." By contrast, Shinto which derived from the seasonal round of agrarian life, made perfect sense to her. It also provided communal continuity, for it was what the ancestors of her ancestors had practiced.

My journey had finished, but as T. S. Eliot memorably put it, "The end is where we start from." A new journey beckoned, one that I hoped would take me to the country's shrines and the circular mirror that stands at their core. In the magic mirror of the Hidden Christians was concealed a secret image of the crucifixion: within the mirror of Shinto lies the soul of Amaterasu. They are two images of the divine, one universal and one particularist. One speaks of a creator God, the other of an ancestral deity. One is transcendent, the other animist. They seem to have little in common, to epitomize an unbridgeable gap whose consequences were evident in the martyrdoms and persecution of Edo times. The genius of the Hidden Christians was to reconcile the two. As they pass into history, their legacy surely deserves to be cherished.

Notes

As with any work of this nature, I have drawn heavily from previous authors to whom I owe a huge debt of gratitude. In particular I should like to acknowledge translations taken from George Elison's *Deus Destroyed: The Image of Christianity in Early Modern Japan* and Michael Cooper's *They Came to Japan*. Information was also gleaned from the books and articles included in the bibliography, in addition to which I should like to give special mention to a website run by Francis Britto that contains a wealth of authoritative and interesting articles related to the Kirishitan period:

All About Francis Xavier http://pweb.cc.sophia.ac.jp/britto/xavier/

Chapter One (Kagoshima)

Information for this and the next two chapters is based on Georg Schurhammer's monumental work, *Francis Xavier: His Life, His Times (1506–1552)*, vol. III and vol. IV.

Translations from *Tratado* (*Topsy-Turvy*) are adapted from Robin Gill, 2005.

Chapter Two (Yamaguchi)

"I can hardly restrain my tears sometimes," Xavier wrote . . . : translated by Robin Gill, 169.

"As soon as ever these Portuguese arrive . . .": translated by Michael Cooper 1965, 64.

Chapter Three (Azuchi)

"The king of Owari would be about 37 years old, tall, thin, sparsely bearded . . .": translated by Michael Cooper 1965, 93.

"At this the bonze rose up . . .": translated by Michael Cooper 1965, 379.

"Inside the walls are many beautiful and exquisite houses . . . .": translated by Michael Cooper 1965, 134.

"I therefore repeat that it is essential that everybody should show the deepest reverence." translated by Michael Cooper 1965, 102.

"There did not remain even a small hair . . .": translated by Michael Cooper 1965, 163.

Chapter Four (Hakata)

Information for this chapter is drawn from Higashibaba Ikuo, George Elison and the *Cambridge History of Japan* section on "Hideyoshi's anti-Christian edicts." For Valignano's policy of accommodation, I'm indebted to Robin Gill. I'm also grateful to Christopher Spilzman for hosting me during the research.

"I will not permit any man of honor to become a Christian . . .": translated by Diego Yuuki, 23.

"It was in the castle and palace of Juraku that Taiko [Hideyoshi] received . . .": translated by Michael Cooper 1974, 117.

"They excel not only all the other Oriental peoples . . .": translated by Michael Cooper 1965, 4.

"They have but one language and it is the best . . .": translated by Michael Cooper 1965, 171.

Chapter Five (Nagasaki)

Information for this chapter draws heavily on Diego Yuuki's *The Twenty-Six Martyrs of Nagasaki,* from which are drawn the quotations except for "The cross is laid on the ground and the body of the sufferer . . .": translated by Michael Cooper 1965, 157.

Chapter Six (Omura)

I'm indebted to Higashibaba Ikuo for ideas in this and the following chapter. See his *Christianity in Early Modern Japan: Kirishitan Belief and Practice*. Information about Tsuji comes from the Society of Jesus website, and about other Omura martyrs from Giles Milton, 303–305.

The Luis Frois quotation "Now the idol had above it a cockerel . . ." is cited in Stephen Turnbull, *The Samurai Sourcebook* London: Arms and Armour Press, 1998.

"We were Kirishitan for many years . . .": translated by Higashibaba Ikuo, 146.

Endo Shusaku's "It has been my long-held supposition . . . ." comes from "Mothers" ("Haha naru mono"), translated by Van C. Gessel in *The Columbia Anthology of Modern Japanese Literature*.

"Those who having been instructed in the way of Truth . . .": translated by Anesaki Masaharu in "Writings on martyrdom in Kirishitan literature."

"There is no nation on earth that fears death less . . .": translated Michael Cooper 1965, 42.

"Nowhere else in Asia were Christian propagandists able to gain such a ready hearing . . ." is taken from George Sansom, 1950.

Chapter Seven (Shimabara)

Information in this and the following chapter was drawn from the chapter on Amakusa Shiro in *The Nobility of Failure* by Ivan Morris (1988), *Deus Destroyed* by George Elison and *Historical Heritage of Minami Shimabara* published by Minami Shimabara City.

"If we had not destroyed and annihilated them . . ." taken from Geoffrey C. Gunn "The Duarte Correa Manuscript and the Shimabara Rebellion" in *Crossroads: A Journal of Nagasaki History and Culture,* ed. Lane Earns and Brian Burke-Gaffney.

Chapter Eight (Amakusa Islands)

Information about Fukan Fabian is taken from George Elison and "The Battle of the Books: Christian and Anti-Christian Tracts in the Early Seventeenth Century" by Ikuko Midzunoe on Francis Britto's *All About Francis Xavier* website.

Father Guerreiro's report that "nowadays the churches in Japan are decorated . . .": taken from Alexander Curvelo "Nagasaki: An European Artistic City in Early Modern Japan" *Bulletin of Portuguese-Japanese Studies* 2001, vol. 2, 30.

"The first commandment urges disobedience . . .": translated by George Elison, 283.

Chapter Nine (Sotome)

Information about Christovao Ferreira draws on an article by Hubert Cieslik, "The Case of Christovao Ferreira" in *Monumenta Nipponica*, vol. 29, no. 1 (Spring 1974).

"I was baptised against my will . . ." Endo in "Kirishitan and To-day" from Peter Milward, ed. *The Mutual Encounter of East and West, 1492–1992*, 187–197.

Quotations from Endo Shusaku's *Silence* are translated by William Johnston in the 1980 publication. Those from *Deep River* are by Van C. Gessel in the 1996 publication.

Scorsese quotes are taken from the Internet Movie Database website.

Chapter Ten (Goto Islands)

Information for this chapter draws on articles by Christal Whelan: "Loss of the Signified Among the Kakure Kirishitan" and "Religion Concealed: The Kakure Kirhsitan on Narushima."

"Padre, I have been a very sinful person . . .": taken from a lecture by Higashibaba Ikuo.

Chapter Eleven (Urakami)

Petitjean quote "At about a quarter past noon yesterday . . .": from a letter to Father Girard cited in *Guide to Pilgrimage Sites and Churches in Nagasaki,* Nagasaki Bunkensha, 2005, 21.

Iwakura mission quote: "In every municipality in Europe and America...": Robin Gill 2005, 40.

Chapter Twelve (Hirado)

Information in this chapter draws on Stephen Turnbull's *The Kakure Kirishitan of Japan: A Study of their Development, Beliefs and Rituals to the Present Day.* Also an unpublished article by Urabe Tomoyuki, *"The History of the Christian Faith in Hirado."* Information on William Adams and the English factory is taken from Giles Milton's *Samurai William.*

The William Adams quote, "Coming before the king, he viewed me well . . .": taken from a letter by to his wife, quoted on http://en.wikipedia.org/wiki/William_Adams_(sailor).

The John Saris quote, "the picture of Venus with her sonne Cupid, did hang wantonly set out in a large frame . . ,." is from the online edition of *The Voyage of Captain John Saris to Japan, 1613,* ed. Ernest Satow.

The Lawrence Spalink quote, "Few nations on the face of the earth are more resistant . . , " is taken from Michael Hoffman's article "Veil" in the *Japan Times,* Dec. 2007.

Bibliography

Boxer, Charles. *The Christian Century in Japan: 1549–1650*. Berkeley: University of California Press, 1951.

Cary, Otis. *A History of Christianity in Japan*. London: Curzon Press, 1996.

Cieslik, Hubert S. J. "The Case of Christovao Ferreira." *Monumenta Nipponica*, vol. 29, no. 1 (Spring 1974).

Cooper, Michael, ed. *They Came to Japan: An Anthology of European Reports on Japan, 1543–1640*. Michigan Classics in Japanese Studies, number 15. Ann Arbor: Center for Japanese Studies, University of Michigan, 1995.

──────────. *They Came to Japan: An Anthology of European Reports on Japan, 1543-1640*. Berkeley: University of California Press, 1965.

Elison, George. *Deus Destroyed: The Image of Christianity in Early Modern Japan*. Cambridge, Mass.: Harvard University Press, 1973.

Endo, Shusaku *Deep River*. Translated by Van C. Gessel. New York: New Directions, 1996.

──────────. "Kirishitan and Today" In Milward, *The Mutual Encounter of East and West, 1492–1992*: 187–97.

──────────. *Silence*. Translated by William Johnston. Miami, Fl.: Parkwest Publications, 1980.

Gill, Robin and Luis Frois. *Topsy-turvy 1585*. Key Biscayne, Fl.: Paraverse Press, 2005.

Harrington, Ann M. *Japan's Hidden Christians*. Chicago: Loyola Press, 1992.

Higashibaba, Ikuo. *Christianity in Early Modern Japan: Kirishitan Belief and Practice*. Leiden: E.J. Brill, 2001.

McClain, James L., ed. *The Cambridge History of Japan*, vol. IV. With the assistance of J. W. Hall. Cambridge: Cambridge University Press, 1991.

Milward Peter, ed. *The Mutual Encounter of East and West, 1492–1992*. Tokyo: The Renaissance Institute, 1992.

Milton, Giles. *Samurai William: The Adventurer Who Unlocked Japan*. London: Sceptre, 2003.

Miyazaki Kentaro "Hidden Christians in Contemporary Nagasaki." Translated by Brian Burke-Gaffney. In *Crossroads: A Journal of Nagasaki History and Culture*. Nagasaki: Crossroads, 1993.

_____ "The Kakure Kirishitan Tradition." in Mark Mullins, ed. *Handbook of Christianity*. Leiden: E.J. Brill, 2003.

Moran, J. F. *The Japanese and the Jesuits*. London: Routledge, 1993.

Nosco, Peter. "Secrecy and the Transmission of Tradition." *Japanese Journal of Religious Studies*, vol. 20, no. 1 (1993).

Sansom, George. *A History of Japan*. 3 vols. Stanford, CA: Stanford University Press, 1958–63.

_____. *The Western World and Japan*. New York: Alfred A. Knopf, 1950.

Schurhammer Georg, S. J. *Francis Xavier: His Life, His Times (1506–1552)*, vol. III and vol. IV. Rome: Jesuit Historical Institute, 1982.

Turnbull, Stephen. *The Kakure Kirishitan of Japan: A Study of Their Development, Beliefs and Rituals to the Present Day*. Richmond, UK: Japan Library, 1998.

_____, ed. *Japan's Hidden Christians*. Key Papers on Japan. 2 vols. London: Routledge, 2000.

Whelan, Christal. *The Beginnings of Heaven and Earth: The Sacred Book of Japan's Hidden Christians*. Nanzan Library of Asian Religion and Culture. Hawaii: University of Hawaii Press, 1996.

_____. "Loss of the Signified Among the Kakure Kirishitan." *Japanese Religions*, vol. 19, no. 1 and 2 (1994): 82–105.

_____ . "Religion Concealed: The Kakure Kirishitan on Narushima." *Monumenta Nipponica*, vol. 47 (1992): 1–25.

Yuuki, Diego. *The Twenty-Six Martyrs of Nagasaki*. Tokyo: Enderle Books, 1998.